Literacy Instruction in Half- and Whole-Day Kindergarten

Research to Practice

Literacy Instruction in Half- and Whole-Day Kindergarten

Research to Practice

Lesley Mandel Morrow

Dorothy S. Strickland

Deborah Gee Woo

Rutgers
The State University of New Jersey
New Brunswick, New Jersey, USA

INTERNATIONAL
Reading
Association

800 Barksdale Road
PO Box 8139
Newark, Delaware 19714-8139, USA
www.reading.org

NATIONAL READING CONFERENCE

National Reading Conference
122 South Michigan Avenue
Suite 1100
Chicago, Illinois 60603, USA

The International Reading Association attempts, through its publications, to provide a forum for a wide spectrum of opinions on reading. This policy permits divergent viewpoints without implying the endorsement of the Association.

Library of Congress Cataloging in Publication Data
Morrow, Lesley Mandel.
    Literacy instruction in half- and whole-day kindergarten: Research to practice/ Lesley Mandel Morrow, Dorothy S. Strickland, Deborah Gee Woo.
        p.   cm.—(Literacy studies series)
    Includes bibliographical references and index.
    1. Reading (Kindergarten)—United States.   2. Literacy—United States.   3. Curriculum planning—United States   4. School day—United States   5. Full-day kindergarten—United States.   I. Strickland, Dorothy S.   II. Woo, Deborah Gee.   III. Title.   IV. Series.
LB1181.2.M67   1998   98-12319
372.4—dc21
ISBN 0-87207-188-X

Acknowledgments

We are grateful to the many individuals who helped with this research investigation. Thank you to the administrators in the New Brunswick, New Jersey, public schools (Dr. Ronald Larkin, Superintendent, and Dr. Penelope Lattimer, Assistant Superintendent) for allowing us to collect the data. In particular we thank Dr. Timber Washington, principal of the kindergartens involved in the research. We thank the 10 kindergarten teachers for allowing us to observe in their classrooms for the year in which the investigation took place and to test the children selected for the study. We thank the 24 Rutgers students who did the observations in the classrooms and tested the children. We also thank Research Assistant Maureen Melia, who organized the data collection and saw that it was analyzed. We thank Gerilyn Bier who gave extensive assistance with the literature review on half-day and whole-day kindergartens. In addition we thank Dr. John Young from the Rutgers Graduate School of Education's Department of Educational Psychology for his help with the design and analysis of the quantitative data in the study.

This study was funded in part by the National Reading Research Center at the Universities of Maryland and Georgia.

106511

Contents

NOTE FROM THE SERIES EDITORS   viii

FOREWORD   ix

INTRODUCTION

    Literacy Instruction in Half- and   1
    Whole-Day Kindergarten:
    Research to Practice

CHAPTER 1

    Issues Concerning Half-Day and   5
    Whole-Day Kindergarten Programs

CHAPTER 2

    The Purpose of the Study, Methods,   17
    and Procedures

CHAPTER 3

    Results of the Quantitative and   27
    Qualitative Analysis
    (written by the authors with John Young)

CHAPTER 4

    Discussion of Results: Implications of the   49
    Data Analysis for Classroom Practice

CHAPTER 5

    Emergent Literacy Perspectives: 56
    Research to Practice

CHAPTER 6

    A Framework for the Literacy Curriculum   71

CHAPTER 7

    A Framework for Integrating Literacy   87
    Into Content-Area Teaching

CHAPTER 8

    Creating a Framework for Literacy-Rich   98
    Environments

CHAPTER 9

    Planning the Day: Organizing for   112
    Whole-Day and Half-Day Instruction

AFTERWORD   128

APPENDIX A:

    Incorporating a Unit on Nutrition   130

APPENDIX B:

    Assessment Measures From the   153
    Research Study

APPENDIX C:

    Samples of Categorized Anecdotal   169
    Observations Collected for the Study

REFERENCES   180

AUTHOR INDEX   189

SUBJECT INDEX   192

Note From the Series Editors

The Literacy Studies Series is intended to advance current knowledge in the field of literacy and to help make research a more important focus in the literacy community. We envision the series as an important professional resource for informing literacy instruction and policy.

Lesley Mandel Morrow, Dorothy S. Strickland, and Deborah Gee Woo, who are well respected for their previous work in early literacy education, have fulfilled this purpose by studying both whole- and half-day kindergarten programs to determine the types of literacy activities that occurred and the amount of time spent on these activities. The authors address a number of questions significant to literacy professionals including: What is the best way to begin early literacy instruction? How much time should be spent on literacy instruction in kindergarten classrooms? Should kindergarten meet for a full school day?

We selected *Literacy Instruction in Half- and Whole-Day Kindergarten* for the Literacy Studies Series because it helps us answer these and other important questions about kindergarten literacy practices. We hope that this volume will play the role of informing teachers, researchers, and the larger educational community about appropriate and "best" practices in kindergarten. It seems that the ongoing debate about the effectiveness of half-day versus full-day kindergarten may best be determined by examining the literacy practices that exist within each program. The authors of this book did so.

James Flood and Diane Lapp, Series Editors
San Diego State University,

Foreword

Kindergarten represents a transition year in children's lives. Moving from the protective settings of home and preschool, children enter a new social world in kindergarten that is filled with unfamiliar adults, regulations, and routines. During this year, the teaching and learning processes so natural and informal in home and neighborhood settings will give way to more systematic and structured instruction. The time devoted to play and physical activity will often compete with time for more formal subject-area learning.

The stakes are high in this transition year. Expectations of what children will need to know by the end of kindergarten have changed dramatically in recent years. Today, in addition to socialization, the traditional emphasis in kindergarten, crucial skills of learning to read and write are the focus of the curriculum. It is now expected that children will learn about critical concepts of print and how our alphabetic system works, and will have had many opportunities to use oral and written language to express meaning and share experiences with others.

Many children entering kindergarten, however, will have very different levels of knowledge about written language. Instruction will need to be adapted for these differences. For those children with a good deal of print experience, instruction will take on more about the formal features of letters and their sound correspondences. For children with fewer prior experiences, the focus of instruction will be initiating them to the alphabetic principle, the fact that symbols make up the alphabet and stand for at least one sound. In all cases, however, children will need to engage and interact with a rich variety of print. Thus, an essential feature of all good teaching, but particularly important for the essential feature of all good teaching, but particularly important for the kindergarten teacher, will be to estimate each student's experience, to build on that base, and to provide for the highest quality of literacy instruction possible.

Lesley Mandel Morrow, Dorothy S. Strickland, and Deborah Gee Woo report on an essential characteristic of a high-quality kindergarten, the length of the school day. They ask if a whole-day kindergarten program rich in language and literacy experiences impacts children's learning more than a half-day program. The answer, as they explain in this book, is a resounding *yes*. High-quality whole-day programs do make a difference: They provide a more intensive, ongoing, enriched language and literacy experience for the young child.

Not only are these basic questions about the length of school day answered in this analysis, but this book is particularly helpful because that research evidence also is accompanied with specific, targeted examples of language and literacy activities. Further, the authors provide models that display how language and literacy activities may thread throughout the curriculum so as not to take away from any other essential part of children's early experiences, like play. As a result, teachers and policymakers will find both qualitative and quantitative evidence to suggest that a balanced, developmentally appropriate language and literacy curriculum is not only beneficial, but perhaps crucial, in these early years.

This book marks an exciting new collaboration for the International Reading Association and the National Reading Conference. These two organizations have joined together for a book series designed to promote greater access to literacy research and best practice. And what better way to begin the series than with a focus on early literacy practices in kindergarten.

Susan B. Neuman
Temple University
Philadelphia, Pennsylvania, USA
Chair of Publications
National Reading Conference

Literacy Instruction in Half- and Whole-Day Kindergarten: Research to Practice

This book discusses issues concerning literacy instruction in kindergarten and more specifically the issues surrounding whole-day and half-day programs. We have spent many years studying emergent literacy through our own research and through the work of others. Our goal was to interpret our own and others' findings into practice. We also have done extensive staff development in schools in the area of early literacy development, observing both whole-day and half-day classes.

Because of our research we were asked by an urban school district in New Jersey to carry out staff development for all of the kindergarten teachers. The district had been involved in redesigning its kindergarten curriculum to use an emergent literacy perspective rather than a reading-readiness approach and to include elements of an integrated language arts program.

With these changes in mind, teachers in the district had written thematic units to help integrate all aspects of the kindergarten curriculum. But the teachers and administrators had many concerns with the changes that were about to take place, including issues such as strategies and organizational management for skill development, use of literature to develop concepts about books and comprehension of text, oral language and writing development, assessment strategies, and the design of centers in their classrooms to support the new instructional framework.

Teachers and administrators were committed to using practices that were developmentally appropriate for kindergarten children, but at the same time, the district had made a decision to change from half- to whole-day kindergarten in five of its schools. The rest of the kindergartens would remain as half-day programs. Administrators wanted to pilot whole-day kindergarten programs but did not have the resources to convert all of their kindergartens from half to whole day simultaneously.

In collaboration with the district's director of staff development, we planned several sessions about developmentally appropriate practice and strategies for literacy development that included integrating the language arts and constructivist and direct instructional strategies for enhancing skills and understanding. We worked with teachers who would be in half- and whole-day programs. We addressed various topics including preparing literacy-rich classroom environments, storybook reading strategies, writing, word analysis, developing comprehension of text, assessment techniques and organizing and managing the school day.While we were involved in the staff development, the issue of whole-day versus half-day kindergarten was very much on the minds of the teachers. Some teachers who were moving into whole-day programs after many years in half-day classrooms were concerned about what they would do with the extra time. Others were excited about the prospect of having more time available to include the experiences they felt had been neglected due to the half-day schedule. Some of the half-day teachers wished they were changing to the whole-day program and others felt relieved that they did not have to change or be the first ones to change.

It became apparent that there were several issues to study concerning the changes that were occurring in the kindergartens where we were working. Taking the teachers' concerns and the staff development into consideration, we decided to investigate the types of literacy activities that occurred and the amount of time spent on literacy activities in the whole-day and half-day kindergarten programs. We also wanted to determine the effect that these programs had on the literacy achievement of children in these inner-city schools. We planned the study to investigate these issues and to determine if there were differences in the literacy activities or in the proportion of time spent in the activities in the whole-day and half-day programs. This

2

there were differences in the literacy activities or in the proportion of time spent in the activities in the whole-day and half-day programs. This was of particular interest because all teachers had the same staff development. In addition to achievement, we were interested in teachers' attitudes and the attitudes of children toward whole-day and half-day programs.

This book is a result of our examinations and is written for those interested in research and practice in early literacy instruction, particularly in kindergarten. We present a research study based on emergent-literacy perspectives for literacy development. The purpose of the study was to determine the effect of whole-day and half-day kindergarten on the literacy achievement of children in inner-city schools. We were interested to find out about literacy activities that occurred in the two settings as well as the attitudes of teachers and children about half- and whole-day programs.

The results of the study revealed that the length of the school day did have an effect on literacy achievement. Equally important were findings about the practices within the half- and whole-day classrooms. Based on our extensive observations during the study, we discuss frameworks for designing the literacy curriculum and suggest plans for organizing the classroom in both whole-day and half-day kindergartens.

In Chapter 1 we discuss the history of and issues concerning whole-day and half-day kindergarten programs. Chapter 2 presents the methods and procedures used to carry out the investigation, and Chapter 3 describes both the quantitative and qualitative data collected. Chapter 4 summarizes the results of the study and presents implications for future research and for classroom practice. The second part of the book focuses on practice drawn from the research. Chapter 5 presents perspectives on early literacy development, Chapter 6 provides a framework for the literacy curriculum with an emphasis on skill development, and Chapter 7 continues to expand on the curriculum framework by discussing a program for integrating content-area subjects and literacy development throughout the school day using thematic instruction. In Chapter 8, we describe a framework for the physical design of classrooms that is necessary to support the planned curriculum. Chapter 9 presents a detailed daily plan for implementing, organizing, and integrating the framework into whole-day and half-day kindergarten programs.

Three appendixes are included at the end of the book. Appendix A presents an entire thematic unit that demonstrates how literacy instruction can be integrated into the total kindergarten day throughout all content areas, illustrating the framework for the curriculum discussed in the text. The assessment measures from the research investigation, and examples of additional anecdotes from the qualitative data that illustrate types of literacy activities that occurred in the whole-day and half-day programs are presented in Appendix B and C.

This book presents research about literacy instruction and also provides a program for kindergarten instruction using an emergent literacy, developmentally appropriate practice, and an integrated language arts perspective. It answers many of the questions that the teachers we worked with had about the new programs and the issues they had with half-day and whole-day programs. It also leaves many questions unanswered and offers suggestions for future research. The book was designed to speak to many individuals, including classroom teachers, supervisors of reading and early childhood programs, and researchers. We hope that this combination of research translated into practice will serve both the research community and the classroom community.

CHAPTER 1

Issues Concerning Half-Day and Whole-Day Kindergarten Programs

The length of the kindergarten day and the corresponding social, emotional, and intellectual benefits for children have long been debated. Proponents and opponents of either half-day or whole-day programs weave a multitude of academic, socioeconomic, and political factors into their arguments. Current concerns for extending the kindergarten day include the belief that academic preparation will contribute to later success in school, and the desire and need for quality early educational environments for all children, especially for children of single parents and in households where both parents work. The increase in the number of children who have whole-day preschool experience prior to kindergarten also makes half-day kindergarten seem inappropriate (Peskin, 1988). Before debating the merits of half-day versus whole-day kindergarten, we will look at the history of kindergarten in an attempt to determine why most kindergartens in the United States are half day.

Historical Perspectives and Kindergarten

Kindergarten, which means "children's garden," was started in Germany in 1837 by philosopher and educator Friedreich Froebel. Froebel believed children should attend kindergarten for the following reasons:

5

To strengthen their bodily powers; to exercise their senses; to employ their awakening mind; to make them thoughtfully acquainted with the world of nature and of man; to guide their heart and soul in the right direction, and lead them to the origin of all life. (Barnard, 1981, p. 91)

Froebel placed a strong emphasis on play. He wrote music, stories, riddles, and games for his kindergarten students. He also developed manipulative materials for learning, which he called "gifts." These materials were designed to teach about colors, shapes and sizes.

Froebel's ideas were first published in the United States in an 1856 pamphlet issued by the *American Journal of Education*. The first U.S. kindergarten was started that year in Watertown, Wisconsin, by Margaret Schurz, a student of Froebel's in Germany. Schurz conducted her program in German for her daughter and the children of friends.

Education advocate Elizabeth Peabody was so impressed by the abilities and behavior of Schurz's daughter that she opened the first English-speaking kindergarten in Boston, Massachusetts, in 1860. Peabody also organized the first teacher training center for kindergarten teachers in the United States and was the chief publicist of the kindergarten movement. Although Peabody was not able to start public-school kindergarten in Boston because of funding problems, she convinced the superintendent of the St. Louis, Missouri, public schools to open the first public-school kindergarten in 1873. Within 6 years, St. Louis had 53 kindergarten classes. By the 1880s, there were hundreds of kindergarten classes in public schools across the United States.

There are conflicting reports regarding the length of the original kindergarten day. According to Puleo (1988), Froebel began kindergarten as a whole-day program. Conversely, Holmes and McConnell (1990) report that Froebel operated his kindergarten for 2 hours in the afternoon and paid little attention to the length of the school day (Bryant & Clifford, 1992).

According to Peskin (1988), kindergarten in the United States began as a whole-day program, but there is varied information about when some programs were reduced to half day. Growth in the student population and lack of funding during the United States's Great Depression motivated many school systems to cut their kindergarten programs to half day because these programs enabled one teacher to accommodate two different groups of children in the same classroom each day. Other explanations of why kindergarten programs became half day were the teacher shortage during World War II and cost and space factors in the 1950s as "baby boomers" began to enter kindergarten in droves. At this time, others believed that 5-year-olds were not mature enough for whole-day school (Holmes & McConnell, 1990; Puleo, 1988).

Whole-day kindergarten programs began to reemerge in the 1960s and 1970s (Oelerich, 1979). This trend seemed to be fueled largely by a new push for academics that stretched from kindergarten through college. Some issues surrounding these "back to the basics" and "catch up" mentalities were the Soviet launch of Sputnik, the publishing of *Why Johnny Can't Read* (Flesch, 1955), and the growing concern about the effects of poverty on young children. Research also had begun to reveal a relation between early school experience and later academic success (Bryant & Clifford, 1992).

The "back to the basics" movement brought reading and math workbooks to kindergarten with a curriculum that incorporated science, social studies, and formal writing instruction (Webster, 1984). Yet the whole-day kindergartens of the 1980s often emphasized skill development to the exclusion of emotional, social, and physiological growth, a trend that is quite different from kindergarten's traditional philosophy of placing emphasis on the "whole child." More recently, however, this traditional philosophy has once again been embraced strongly. Child development experts are not only interested in the intellectual development of the child in the early years but are concerned about the social, emotional, and physical needs as well (Bredekamp, 1987).

Demographics Concerning Kindergarten Attendance and Length of the School Day

According to a 1993 U.S. Census Bureau survey, roughly 45% of the United States's 4.2 million kindergarten children attend whole-day programs (Adams & Bruno, 1993). Attendance has grown at an explosive rate; the number of kindergarten children in whole-day programs was less than 10% in 1969 and more than 30% in 1982 (Holmes & McConnell, 1990). Total kindergarten enrollment increased 36% between 1973 and 1993. The U.S. Census Bureau calculates that approximately 79% of all 5-year-olds are enrolled in kindergarten and that public schools serve 84% of all kindergarten students (Adams & Bruno, 1993).

Despite kindergarten's high rate of attendance, a survey in 1995 showed that kindergarten attendance is not mandatory in most states (U.S. Department of Education, 1996). Only 10 states—Arizona, Missouri, New Mexico, North Dakota, Ohio, Rhode Island, South Carolina, Tennessee, Utah, and Virginia—mandate kindergarten attendance. Whole-day attendance currently is mandated by just four states—Arkansas, Florida, North Dakota, and Virginia—as well as Washington, D.C. Ten other states require their school districts to offer whole-day kindergarten though attendance is not mandatory. Seventeen states do not require their districts to offer any type of kindergarten (U.S. Department of Education, 1996).

Data collected on the distribution of the whole-day kindergarten population reveal that whole-day kindergarten has been most prevalent in high-poverty areas and in schools with a large minority enrollment. In 1993, two thirds of whole-day kindergarten teachers taught in high-poverty areas, while only 29% taught in schools with a low incidence of poverty (Rothenberg, 1995). Districts with students from minority and low socioeconomic backgrounds often are identified as at risk and receive state and federal funding that they use to create whole-day kindergarten programs (Fromberg, 1992; Housden & Kam, 1992). Whole-day kindergarten also has been prevalent in rural districts because it eliminates the need to pay for busing and crossing guards at midday where children have to travel long distances to get to school.

Renewed Interest in Whole-Day Kindergarten

The widespread return to whole-day kindergarten, like the switch to half-day kindergarten decades ago, has its roots in economic and social changes (Peskin, 1988). The reemergence of whole-day kindergarten is attributed largely to changing family patterns such as single-parent families and households where both parents work. Other reasons for having whole-day kindergarten are a growing desire for quality day care in an educational environment, an increase in the number of children who have attended preschool or day care prior to kindergarten in whole-day settings, and an interest in academic preparation for later school success (Peskin, 1988).

The number of women in the workforce with children under 6 years old has grown rapidly since 1960 (U.S. Department of Commerce, 1995). A majority, 59.6%, of married mothers (husband present) of children under 6 were in the workforce in 1993, up from just 18.6% in 1960. Participation in the workforce for widowed, divorced, or separated mothers of children under 6 also climbed significantly to 60% in 1993, up from 40.5% in 1960. The percentage of single mothers of children under 6 who were in the workforce in 1993 was 47.4%. Nearly 40% of the 3- to 5-year-olds in nursery school and kindergarten have mothers who work full time (U.S. Department of Commerce, 1995).

It is important to look at nursery-school and preschool data because these numbers reveal a great deal about the kindergarten population. Nursery school enrollment jumped 128% between 1973 and 1993, while the number of children in the eligible age group rose by just one sixth. Children whose mothers are in the workforce are more likely to attend whole-day nursery school programs: 43.5% versus 20.3% of all children enrolled (Adams & Bruno, 1993). In addition, today's children are more sophisticated and more verbal as a result of having better-educated parents and a generally higher standard of living (Peskin, 1988).

There are a number of other economic issues influencing the implementation of whole-day kindergarten. First, many states provide more money to local districts for whole-day students than for half-day students. Second, as mentioned earlier, eliminating midday busing saves money (Holmes & McConnell, 1990). In addition, the decline in national enrollment gives some schools space to accommodate whole-day programs (Holmes & McConnell, 1990; Puleo, 1988).

Many educators have pushed for whole-day kindergarten. They emphasize the acquisition of basic skills and the value of providing teachers with additional time to address individual students' needs (Gilstrap, 1970; Gorton & Robinson, 1968; Ross, 1976). Educators also hope that whole-day kindergarten may help reduce grade retention and the need for placing students in special education classes and remedial programs (Herman, 1984).

Theoretical Framework for Instructional Practices in Whole-Day Kindergarten

Quality whole-day kindergarten programs obviously must meet the needs of children beyond providing extended babysitting services. The National Association for the Education of Young Children (NAEYC) has published statements on developmentally appropriate practices that apply to kindergarten students (Bredekamp & Copple, 1997). Appropriate and inappropriate practices are listed for such components as curriculum goals, teaching strategies, guidance of social-emotional development, language development and literacy, integrated curriculum, cognitive development, physical development, aesthetic development, motivation, parent-teacher relations, assessment strategies, teacher qualifications, and staffing.

NAEYC currently has no position on what is the appropriate length of day for kindergarten programs because it believes that this does not determine the quality of a program. The NAEYC publication *Kindergarten Policies—What Is Best for Children?* says, "It appears that we have been asking the wrong question about the length of the kindergarten day...we need to focus on the question, how much time is needed for teachers to offer an appropriate curriculum?" (Peck, Mc-Caig, & Sapp, 1988, p. 63). However, the NAEYC says that if kindergarten programs are developmentally appropriate, it does appear that longer days increase the chance that both long-term and short-term goals for children will be achieved (Fromberg, 1986; Herman, 1984; Naron, 1981).

A major benefit of a longer kindergarten day is that it allows teachers to get to know their students better. The longer day gives teachers the opportunity to develop a more complete and more multi-faceted program. Children can get more involved in the planning of activities because there is more flexibility in the daily schedule. Process-oriented activities, which often require extended time, may be scheduled in large blocks. This is consistent with the work of major learning theorists suggesting that large blocks of time are required for optimal learning conditions during the early years.

For example, the work of Piaget (1969), Vygotsky (1981), and Peck et al. (1988) indicates that spontaneous play, active involvement, and social interaction are critical elements of a young child's learning environment. Peck et al. stressed the importance of providing opportunities for learning through children's spontaneous play. Piaget's theory of cognitive development is based on the principle that children develop through active involvement in learning. Vygotsky's general theory of intellectual development also has implications for learning in early childhood. Vygotsky believed that mental functions are acquired through social relationships in which adults scaffold for children when necessary, stepping back at the appropriate time and allowing youngsters to internalize activities, emulate behaviors, and incorporate them into existing structures of knowledge. Providing opportunities for this type of process learning requires large blocks of time for exploration, and a variety of experiences and materials. This is not always possible in the constraints of a half-day program.

Linking theories such as those mentioned in the previous paragraph to literacy development leads to the notion that learning experiences in kindergarten should be designed to be meaningful and functional for children. Literacy activities should be integrated into content-area subjects such as art, music, social studies, science, math, and play through the use of thematic instruction, with equal emphasis placed on the teaching of reading, writing, listening, and oral language. Varied genres of children's literature can be a main source of reading materials, and classrooms should be rich with literacy materials for reading and writing that are housed in centers for literacy and other content areas. Teachers should provide models of literacy activities for children to emulate, encouraging adult and peer interaction as children observe one another and adults engaged in literacy acts. Opportunities for peer tutoring and collaboration and time to practice skills learned should be provided. Skills should be taught in an organized fashion within relevant and meaningful contexts and when the need arises. Assessment is continuous with the use of multiple authentic measures. Literacy learning should be consciously embedded throughout the curriculum in the entire school day with large blocks of time used for literacy projects (Morrow, 1997). Whole-day kindergarten enables children to engage in projects that take time to complete and can be left unfinished for the next day. Longer kindergarten days also may provide another type of continuity by reducing the number of different child-care programs students have to attend while their parents work. In addition, working parents have a greater opportunity to get involved in school activities because a longer school day provides greater flexibility when scheduling class visits (Peck et al., 1988). However, although numerous practical and theoretical reasons exist to support whole-day kindergarten, these programs must meet the NAEYC standards for developmentally appropriate practice and have a strong theoretical framework for early childhood learning. It is clear that a developmentally appropriate curriculum is the most important element in planning a kindergarten program. After such a curriculum is planned, discussion concerning the length of the school day can then be considered (Karweit, 1992; Peck et al., 1988; Rothenberg, 1995).

A Review of Research Relating to Whole-Day and Half-Day Kindergarten Programs

The results of many of the studies conducted on the length of the kindergarten day favor whole-day over half-day programs, although some studies have found no difference between the two types of kindergartens. There are few studies that favor half-day over whole-day programs. Research has examined the effect of whole-day kindergarten on areas such as basic academic skills, long-term academic performance, instructional methods, social development, emotional development, and attendance patterns. Investigations concerning parent and teacher attitudes toward half-day and whole-day programs also have been conducted. Overall, however, research on whole-day kindergarten is far from definitive. Many experts complain about inadequacies with existing studies and stress the need for additional research.

Puleo (1988) reviewed 19 studies reporting the effects that kindergarten programs of varying lengths had on various basic skills, such as knowledge of letters, sounds, colors, numbers and other variables, such as motivation and self-esteem. All of the studies reported differences in favor of whole-day or extended-day kindergarten programs on all or some of the variables studied, and none of them favored half-day programs.

Several studies provide evidence of long-term academic benefits for children who have attended whole-day kindergarten. Researchers have found that children in whole-day programs performed significantly better in school at the end of Grade 1 and at the end of Grades

3 and 4 (Humphrey, 1980, 1983). Other researchers have obtained favorable findings in third-grade achievement and scholastic aptitude. Long-lasting gains were reported by Nieman and Gastright (1981) who looked at fourth- and eighth-grade students' reading and math achievement. They found that students in both grades who had attended whole-day kindergarten scored significantly higher than students who had attended half-day programs.

Cryan, Sheehan, Wiechel, and Bandy-Hedden (1992) performed a statewide longitudinal study in Ohio that looked at the effects of different kindergarten schedules (whole-day, half-day, and whole-day–alternate-day) on achievement, classroom behavior, incidence of grade retention, and the need for special-education services. The study found that the first-grade test performance of children who attended whole-day kindergarten was superior to that of children who had been in half-day programs. Whole-day students experienced fewer grade retention and fewer Chapter 1 (U.S. federally funded education program for at-risk children now called Title I) placements. When students in whole-day programs were compared with their half-day peers, they exhibited greater levels of productivity and independent learning. They also demonstrated more intellectual independence and less failure and anxiety, and were more reflective in their academic work. Teachers said that these students engaged in less irrelevant talk and exhibited more positive feelings about school. These students also were rated as less withdrawn and as more likely to approach the teacher for help.

Studies also indicate that the largest group of students who are consistent beneficiaries from whole-day kindergarten programs are the academically at-risk children. Reports from New York City's whole-day kindergarten program, which began in 1983, found that the most dramatic gains were made by students from non-English-speaking families (Peskin, 1988).

Harrison-McEachern (1989) conducted a study that compared reading achievement of first-grade students who had attended whole-day and half-day programs in Newark, New Jersey, a district with a large percentage of at-risk students. The students were given the Comprehensive Tests of Basic Skills (CTBS) after 8 months in first grade. Those who attended the whole-day kindergarten program scored significantly higher in reading achievement based on the CTBS.

Holmes and McConnell (1990) tried to determine the academic differences between students attending whole-day (326 students) and half-day (311 students) kindergarten from schools in Title I districts and schools in affluent areas. The researchers looked at six measures of academic achievement from the California Achievement Test that the students took in the spring of their kindergarten year. The test measured visual recognition, sound recognition, vocabulary, comprehension, language expression, and mathematics concepts and applications. Significant differences favoring children in the whole-day programs were obtained on two of the measures: comprehension and math.

Towers (1991) reported on a study concerning parent and teacher reactions to whole-day kindergarten. Questionnaires were sent to families whose children had attended whole-day kindergarten. Of the 85% who responded, 83% felt that their children were better prepared for first grade than if they had attended half-day kindergarten and 75% of the families felt that their children had benefited socially from the whole-day program. The six teachers involved in the whole-day kindergartens were all in favor of the program in terms of the social and emotional benefits it provided students.

As mentioned, not all studies find favor with whole-day kindergarten. Terens (1984) found that half-day kindergartens provided more quality teaching time than did whole-day programs. Children studied in whole-day programs were not able to adapt physically and psychologically to the additional time in school. By the last hour of class, children were tired, restless, hyperactive, or inattentive.

Research Limitations and Implications

What kinds of problems exist with the research on whole-day kindergarten? Many early-childhood experts feel that the quality of research on whole-day kindergarten has not been scientifically rigorous and that it is therefore premature to determine if the findings are as positive as studies have reported. Although there has been growth in more substantial research on whole-day kindergarten in recent years, experts continue to believe that it is still too limited in both quality and quantity (Hatcher, 1990; Karweit, 1992; Peskin, 1988; Puleo, 1988; Walsh, 1989). Demand is particularly great for more longitudinal research.

Another problem with the existing research in this area is that much of it has been conducted by individual districts that employ different methodologies and have different goals and needs. In addition, many studies on whole- and half-day kindergarten have employed only standardized tests to assess children's academic abilities. Hatcher and Schmidt (1990) suggest that a broader range of variables needs to be assessed to determine the impact of whole-day kindergarten programs. Some areas that need to be examined are a kindergarten student's ability to observe, discover, generalize, experiment, and solve problems as a result of attendance in both whole- and half-day classes. Whole- and half-day students' ability to express thoughts and feelings more creatively through language, movement, music, and art also need to be compared. The researchers also suggest examining qualities such as independence, creativity, and self-discipline. In addition, we need to know if different populations benefit more from whole-day programs. We also need to assess academic skills with measures that match more current strategies for instruction and that are considered to be developmentally appropriate. To accomplish this, more authentic assessment tools should be used than have been used in the past.

Other variables that need to be studied include the kindergarten curriculum, class size, socioeconomic status, student attendance patterns, education of parents, and cultural values. The instructional strategies used by teachers and the effect of increased instructional time are of concern because data related to these variables are inconclusive. Synthesizing research findings about whole-day and half-day kindergarten according to variables would enable others to build and improve on what already has been done (Puleo, 1988). Finally, much of the research on the length of the kindergarten day is from the 1970s and 1980s, and we need to investigate this important issue as it related to current instruction.

Conclusion

There are many substantive reasons for supporting whole-day kindergarten. However, additional research needs to be conducted with the appropriate scientific rigor to develop a better understanding of when, where, how, and with what populations such programs should be implemented. We planned the research study presented in this text based on the findings of the literature review and our work with a school district that changed some of its classrooms from half-day to whole-day kindergarten. In this investigation we studied the effect of whole-day and half-day kindergarten programs with specific concern on literacy achievement, instructional strategies used in literacy development, and instructional time spent in this area of the curriculum. The study builds on previous investigations and moves forward to focus on developmentally appropriate strategies for early literacy instruction and on the effects with at-risk children from minority backgrounds in an urban setting. The research design has been constructed carefully and authentic assessment measures have been used to determine gains in achievement. The variables studied in the investigation have been long-standing issues of concern in whole-day and half-day kindergarten research. Although one study cannot answer all of the remaining questions about half-day versus whole-day kindergarten, our goal was to contribute to the ongoing research and debate.

CHAPTER 2

The Purpose of the Study, Methods, and Procedures

As is evident in the preceding chapter, the length of the kindergarten day; the types of developmentally appropriate practice; and the corresponding social, emotional, and intellectual benefits for children have been debated. Proponents of both half-day and whole-day programs discuss academic, socioeconomic, and political factors. There is conflicting evidence about the benefits of whole-day versus half-day programs and questions about the rigor of the research thus far. Therefore we decided to study the issue again to determine the effects of the length of the program on literacy development. Currently schools emphasize early literacy achievement because educators and administrators have come to realize that early success is likely to yield lifelong success. The time we spend on literacy development in school and the nature of the activities carried out during that time is an important question on which to focus.

Purpose of the Study

Our goal was to determine the effect of whole-day and half-day kindergarten on the literacy achievement of children in inner-city schools. In addition we wanted to describe the types of literacy activities that occurred in the whole-day and half-day programs and the amount of time spent on these activities. With these factors in mind, we asked the following specific questions:

1. What types of literacy activities occur in whole-day and half-day programs and what differences are there in these activities?

2. How much time is spent on literacy activities in half-day and whole-day kindergarten classrooms and what proportion of time is spent on literacy in each program?

3. What is the impact of whole-day and half-day programs on the literacy achievement of children in these classrooms?

4. What are the attitudes of teachers and children toward whole-day and half-day kindergarten programs?

Methods of the Study

Subjects

Five half-day and five whole-day kindergarten classrooms in one urban school district were selected randomly for the investigation. The district was moving from half-day to whole-day kindergarten and had been piloting programs by gradually changing some of its kindergartens to whole day. Four girls and four boys were selected randomly as subjects from each of the classrooms for the analysis of literacy achievement. At the end of the study there were data for 36 children in whole-day programs and 30 in half-day programs. Of the 36 children in the whole-day program, 17 were girls and 19 were boys; in the half-day program, 17 children were girls and 13 were boys.

Ninety-five percent of the children in the study were from minority backgrounds (African American and Latino), and 5% were Caucasian. All teachers in the study were experienced; the whole-day teachers had from 10 to 25 years of teaching experience, and the half-day teachers had from 15 to 28 years of teaching experience. All had taught kindergarten in their present setting prior to the study. Most had taught other grades as well.

Procedures

Data collection began in October, during the preintervention stage of the study. From November through April, classrooms were observed twice a month for the entire day to record the types of literacy activities teachers initiated and the number of minutes children were engaged in these literacy activities. There were a total of 12 observations in each room.

The following measures were administered to the children in the study: a Probed Recall Listening Comprehension Test, a Story Retelling Test, a Writing Sample Test, a Story Reenactment Test, a Kindergarten Inventory of Concepts About Print, and Teacher Ratings of Children's Interest and Ability in Reading and Writing. Teachers and children were interviewed concerning their attitudes toward whole-day and half-day programs. In May all of the pretest measures were administered again as posttests, some individually and some in groups. The tests were used to determine literacy achievement and interest in reading and writing. Copies of the assessment measures and interview questions appear in Appendix B.

PROBED RECALL LISTENING COMPREHENSION TEST.   This test was administered by research assistants individually after reading the story *Arthur's Eyes* (Brown, 1979) to a child. The posttest book was *Franklin in the Dark* (Bourgeois, 1986). These books were chosen for quality of plot structure, including strongly delineated characters, definite setting, clear theme, obvious plot episodes, and definite resolution. They were similar in number of pages and words. Testing books were selected with attention to research on children's preferences in books (Monson & Sebesta, 1991). The test included eight traditional comprehension questions focusing on detail, cause and effect, inference, and making critical judgments, plus eight questions focusing on story structure that dealt with setting, theme, plot episodes, and resolution. Research assistants read the questions and recorded children's answers. This instrument was reliable in the range of 92% in previous research with children from similar diverse backgrounds (Morrow, O'Connor, & Smith, 1990; Morrow & Smith, 1990). In this study six coders scored the five pretests and posttests with 92% agreement.

STORY RETELLING TEST.   This test was used because it is a holistic measure of comprehension that demonstrates retention of facts, as well as the ability to construct meaning by retelling text. The test measures literal knowledge of stories, specific elements of story structure, and story sequencing. The same storybooks were used in this test as were used on the Listening Comprehension Test.

Research assistants administered the Story Retelling Tests on an individual basis. When taking the test, children listen to a story that is read to them. They are asked to retell it as if they are doing it for a friend who had never heard the story before. In the tape-recorded oral retelling, prompts are limited to "Then what happened?" or "What comes next?" Story retellings are then evaluated for the inclusion of setting, theme, plot episodes, and resolution. A child received credit for partial recall or for understanding the important elements of a story event (Pellegrini & Galda, 1982; Thorndyke, 1977). The scorers observed sequence by comparing the order of events in the child's retelling with that in the original by constructing a meaningful presentation. The interrater reliability of the scoring scheme (roughly 90%) and the overall validity of the measures have been established in previous investigations with children from diverse backgrounds (Morrow, 1992; Morrow & Smith, 1990). For this study, seven coders scored six protocols with 92% agreement for story retellings.

WRITING SAMPLE TEST.   For this test, children were asked to draw a picture about their family, a television show they liked, or something special to them. The research assistant helped the children decide what they would draw if they could not decide alone, telling the children that they would be asked to write something about their picture. If children said they could not write, they were told that they could "pretend write", and were shown samples of children's scribble writing, letter-like forms, letter strings, and invented spellings. After the children drew the pictures they wrote about them. Using Sulzby's (1986) broad categories of writing, we rated children's samples from one to six. Our ratings were based on the following categories: writing via drawing, writing via scribbling, writing via letter-like forms, writing via reproducing well-learned letter strings, writing via invented spelling, and writing via conventional spelling. In this study six coders scored the five pretests and posttests with 97% agreement.

STORY REENACTMENT TEST.   This test asked children to read a story that was well known to them. The child knew the story well and if he or she was not yet a conventional reader, could pretend read the story. If the child voiced an inability to read, the research assistant told him or her to pretend read by looking at the pictures or the words and telling the story as if he or she were reading, because the story was familiar from hearing it many times before. Using Sulzby's (1985) reenactment categories, children's story readings were rated for the following characteristics: picture governed, story not well formed;

picture governed, story well formed, and sounds like a storytelling presentation; picture governed, story well formed, presentation mixed to sound part like storytelling and part as if the story was being read; picture governed, story well formed, sounds like the story was being read; and print governed, child read the story. Six coders scored six pretests and posttests with 90% agreement.

KINDERGARTEN INVENTORY OF CONCEPTS ABOUT PRINT. This inventory, adapted from work by Marie Clay (1985), tested children's knowledge about print such as identification of letters, words, and concepts about books including being able to identify the front and back of a book, the title, and the author.

TEACHER RATINGS OF CHILDREN'S INTEREST AND ABILITY IN READING AND WRITING. Teacher ratings were measured on a scale from one to five, with one being the lowest and five the highest. This measure served as a way of determining increased achievement and motivation or interest in reading and writing.

Collecting the Observational Data

From November through April, research assistants observed in the five half-day and five whole-day classrooms, twice a month for a total of 12 observations per room. They observed for the entire day and recorded the types of literacy activities initiated and carried out by teachers and the time spent on each activity.

Prior to the classroom visits, research assistants participated in training sessions discussing the types of activities they were likely to see and how they were to record their observations. Students observed and recorded data in practice sessions to be sure they understood the data-collection procedures. We observed videotapes of kindergartens and made on-site visits to record literacy activities and the amount of time spent on each activity, ensuring that the data were being collected in the same manner. The observation data were collected on forms prepared to reflect the description of literacy activities, the location of the activities, the organizational structure (whole group, small group, one on one, teacher directed, or independent), and the number of minutes spent on the activity. The guidesheets developed for the research assistants included instructions on how to observe in an educational setting and how to focus on the behaviors of children and teachers during literacy activities. Copies of these forms also appear in Appendix B.

Data collection proceeded through two phases (Corsaro, 1985; Lincoln & Guba, 1985). First, observers familiarized themselves with the children and the teachers and established their roles as individuals collecting field notes in the classrooms. The first set of field notes provided an initial source for evaluating data quality. These notes also helped to refine and standardize the procedures, thus assuring that the kinds of data sought actually were being collected. The second phase involved the collection of data based on the refined procedures for taking field notes. Students were to identify and record all teacher-initiated literacy activities observed.

Another phase of data collection occurred after the categories of activities were identified. Observers went back into the classroom to record complete descriptions of each type of literacy activity. This second set of field notes followed activities from beginning to end and included dialogue between teachers and children. They also included organizational structures used, children's names and genders, materials used, as well as the roles and actions of teachers and children (Bogdan & Biklen, 1982; Fetterman, 1984; Green & Wallat, 1981). This type of notetaking is referred to by Barker (1963) as the stream of behavior chronicle because it records minute-by-minute what subjects do and say.

In addition to the observational data, teachers and children were interviewed to determine their attitudes toward whole-day and half-day programs.

The Kindergarten Program

The district in which this study took place was gradually changing from half-day kindergartens to whole-day programs. There was also an effort to improve instruction in all kindergartens regardless of length of day. A committee of kindergarten teachers wrote a new curriculum for the district with the intent to implement a developmentally appropriate program using an integrated language arts approach in literacy, and thematic instruction to achieve an integrated school day. The goals section of the kindergarten curriculum manual included the following suggestions:

1. Provide a learning environment for children that will help them develop intellectually, socially, physically, and emotionally in a manner appropriate to their age and stage of development.
2. Integrate the educational concepts of health, social, and emotional well being into a varied daily program of activities.
3. Enhance children's feelings of self-worth and appreciation of their own and others' ethnicity, culture, and language in a multicultural society.
4. Develop social competence by providing opportunities for children to make decisions and solve problems during the school day.
5. Provide for prevention, early identification, and early intervention of problems that interfere with the development of children's learning.
6. Stress concrete, hands-on, multisensory experiences.
7. Provide rich experiences that foster skills in listening, speaking, emergent writing, emergent reading, and literature appreciation.
8. Include a balance of teacher-directed and child-initiated activities that offer choices for children.
9. Use an integrated curriculum through thematic units.
10. Select teachers and support personnel who have strong educational and experiential backgrounds in early-childhood education and child development, and enhance their skills with frequent staff-development programs.

With these goals in mind, all of the kindergarten teachers who were involved in this study participated in staff-development sessions that we provided. The sessions dealt with developmentally appropriate practice and integrated language arts strategies for literacy development. The teachers studied the design and use of literacy centers and other content-area centers in kindergarten classrooms. They also looked at various strategies including storybook reading, writing strategies, and strategies for developing comprehension skills such as story retelling, strategies for word analysis, and authentic assessment. They learned how to integrate the curriculum with content-area themes and embed literacy into content-area teaching. Finally they learned how to organize literacy experiences with whole-group, small-group, and one-on-one instruction, and with teacher-directed and student-initiated activities.

The curriculum prepared by the teachers contained a range of skills aimed at developing literacy that included listening, speaking, and emergent and conventional reading and writing. The manual covered about 50 objectives. This material was integrated into thematic units written by the teachers that included topics such as Family, Mostly Me: Our Bodies (self-esteem), Friends, What's for Lunch? (nutrition), Transportation, Pet Show, Plants, Spring, Ecology/Pollution, Fire Safety, The Sea, and African American History (Washington, Lee, Thomson, Moomgy, & Gable, 1993).

An outline for a school day was developed with the teachers for both whole-day and half-day programs. However, individuals had the freedom to rearrange their days to suit their teaching styles and the needs of their children. The district felt that there was no one daily routine that had to be established for all kindergarten classrooms. However, there was a basic model with blocks of time set aside for categories of activities to be included. The tone, content, and strategies for learning that occurred in these time periods were far more important than adherence to one specific schedule. The classroom observations of literacy activities during the data-collection period indicate that three of the teachers in whole-day and three in the half-day programs did implement the plan quite well. One teacher in the half-day and one in the whole-day program did not follow the plan as proposed, and in one other room in both half-day and whole-day programs, teachers did a moderate job of implementation.

Because so many teachers followed the instructional plan, our samples of whole-day and half-day rooms are quite similar. A sample of the guide created with the teachers during staff-development sessions for a half-day and whole-day kindergarten program is outlined in the following sections.

Half-Day Program for a Kindergarten Classroom

8:30 to 9:00

Arrival at school, storage of outdoor clothing, breakfast.

9:00 to 9:30

Morning get-together, opening exercises, morning message, discussion of unit topic, songs or musical movement activities related to unit topic, daily news, planning for the school day.

9:30 to 9:50

Whole-class lesson in language arts, math, social studies, or science, varying from day to day, with an assignment to complete that flows into the next period.

9:50 to 10:10

Small-group or one-on-one conferences dealing with literacy instruction. The rest of the class completes work from the whole-class lesson; children work in designated centers or at their tables with assigned work by the teacher. Children who are not working with the teacher use this time for literacy center activities.

10:10 to 10:35

Center time. All centers are open including art, music, blocks, dramatic play, literacy, science, and social studies. Special projects are set up at the different centers. Children can choose where to work and what activities they will do.

10:35 to 10:50

Clean up and snack.

10:50 to 11:10

Outdoor play, or large motor games in the gymnasium.

11:10 to 11:30

Teacher reads a story to children. Children participate in quiet book reading. Children summarize the school day. Time for quiet book reading. Dismissal.

Whole-Day Program for a Kindergarten Classroom

8:30 to 9:15

Arrival at school, storage of outdoor clothing, breakfast.

9:15 to 9:45

Morning get-together, opening exercises, morning message, discussion of unit topic, songs or musical movement activities related to unit topic, daily news, planning for the school day.

9:45 to 10:15

Whole-class lesson in language arts, math, social studies, or science, varying from day to day, with an assignment to complete that flows into the next period.

10:15 to 10:45

Small-group or one-on-one conferences dealing with literacy instruction. The rest of the class completes work from the whole-class lesson; children work in designated centers or at their tables with assigned work by the teacher. Children not working with the teacher use this time for literacy center activities.

10:45 to 11:15

Center time. All centers are open including art, music, blocks, dramatic play, literacy, science, and social studies. Special projects are set up at the different centers. Children can choose where to work and what activities they will do.

11:15 to 11:30

Clean up and snack.

11:30 to 12:00

Outdoor play, or large motor games in the gymnasium.

12:00 to 1:30

Lunch, bathroom, rest.

1:30 to 1:55

Teacher reads a story to children. Children participate in quiet book reading.

1:55 to 2:20

Center time. All centers are open with a special project in one of the areas. Children can choose where to work and what activities they will do.

2:20 to 2:40

Outdoor play, large motor play in gymnasium, or large motor musical movement activities.

2:40 to 3:00

Circle time to summarize the day's activities, plan for the next day, share items brought from home that are related to the unit, and share work created by students. Sing a song related to the unit of study, read a story. Dismissal.

Although the plans for half- and whole-day kindergarten are similar, they differ in the amount of time spent on activities. In addition, the afternoon provided the opportunity in the whole-day kindergarten for additional projects and activities.

CHAPTER 3

Results of the Quantitative and Qualitative Analysis
(written by the authors with John Young)

Analysis of the Quantitative and Observational Data

After the data had been collected, the following procedures were used for analysis in order to obtain the results. Because the subjects were selected randomly from all classrooms the child was used as a unit of analysis. Achievement data were analyzed using a one-way analysis of covariance with two groups: half-day and whole-day kindergarten.

We reviewed the observational data and analyzed it for types of literacy experiences observed (such as storybook reading) and the number of minutes spent on literacy activities. The approach to data analysis was not strictly inductive because we began with previous knowledge about what literacy activities we might expect to see. It also was not strictly deductive because we wanted to discover activities that might be happening that we had not anticipated. Adapting the constant comparative research procedure used by Miles and Huberman (1984), we reviewed the data and reduced it into categories from which trends emerged concerning literacy activities initiated by teachers. We alternated between macroanalysis in which broad categories emerged and were clarified and microanalysis in which subcategories within the larger ones were listed. The amount of time spent in teacher-initiated literacy activities was recorded (Alvermann, O'Brien, & Dillon, 1990).

To check for observer reliability, five research assistants collected data by recording and coding data into literacy activities and recording the number of minutes spent in these activities. There was 95% agreement concerning types of literacy activities recorded from classroom observations and 90% agreement in the number of minutes spent on activities.

Literacy Achievement Results

Table 1 presents the pretest and posttest means and standard deviations for the literacy achievement measures and the teacher ratings of reading ability. The ANCOVA (analysis of covariance) for the total score on the comprehension measure, $F(1,63) = 4.93, p < .001$, showed that the whole-day kindergarten children scored significantly better than the half-day children. In order to control for initial differences, pretest scores were used as a covariate in the ANCOVA.

The ANCOVA for the total score on Story Retelling, $F(1,56) = 4.27, p < .001$, showed that the whole-day kindergarten children scored significantly better than the half-day children. The ANCOVA for the Writing Samples, $F(1,51) = 4.11, p < .001$, also found that the children in the whole-day kindergarten scored significantly better than those in the half-day programs.

On the Story Reenactment Test the ANCOVA $F(1,64) = 4.62, p < .001$ showed a significant difference between the groups.

The Kindergarten Inventory of Concepts About Print ANCOVA, $F(1,64) = 9.93, p < .001$, found that the children in the whole-day kindergartens once again performed significantly better than children in the half-day kindergartens.

Finally, the teachers' ratings of children's reading ability and interest are recorded on Table 1. The ANCOVA for reading ability, $F(1,55) = 4.78, p < .001$, and for reading interest, $F(1,57) = p < .005$, was significantly different with the whole-day kindergartners being rated higher than the half-day children.

Results From the Observational Data

Categories of Literacy Activities Observed in Whole-Day and Half-Day Kindergartens

Table 2 contains the categories of literacy activities that emerged from the 12 observations in the five whole-day and five half-day

Table 1
Means and Standard Deviations for Literacy Achievement Measures

	Half-Day Kindergartners				Whole-Day Kindergartners			
	Pretest	(SD)	Posttest	(SD)	Pretest	(SD)	Posttest	(SD)
Comprehension	12.33	(5.78)	19.40[a]	(6.57)	9.94	(6.21)	25.25[b]	(7.31)
Story Retelling	4.06	(3.40)	6.42[a]	(3.63)	3.76	(1.99)	9.50[b]	(2.93)
Writing Sample	4.33	(1.30)	3.66[a]	(1.70)	3.76	(1.92)	4.84[b]	(1.31)
Story Reenactment	2.10	(.84)	2.43[a]	(.81)	1.86	(.68)	3.05[b]	(.86)
Teacher Rating of Reading Ability	2.56	(1.94)	2.56[a]	(.93)	2.78	(.62)	3.58[b]	(.62)
Teacher Rating of Reading Interest	3.46	(1.22)	3.55[a]	(1.35)	2.96	(.88)	3.73[b]	(.78)
Kindergarten Inventory	3.76	(1.22)	3.26[a]	(1.50)	2.58	(1.64)	5.66[b]	(.58)

Note: Posttest means are adjusted for pretest scores.

[ab] Posttest scores are significantly different (p < .05) if they do not share the same superscript.

Table 2
Comparison of Total Time, Average Time, and Percentage of Instructional Time Spent in Literacy Activities for Whole-Day and Half-Day Kindergartens

	Total Time (in Minutes)	Average Time (in Minutes)	Percentage of Instructional Time
Whole-Day			
Storybook Activities	2,365	39.4	16%
Comprehension Strategies	660	11	4%
Knowledge About Print	1,875	31	12%
Writing Activities	955	16	6%
Oral Language Activities	1,060	18	7%
Content-Area Literacy	830	14	5%
All Literacy Combined	7,745	129	51%
Half-Day			
Storybook Activities	810	13.5	9%
Comprehension Strategies	330	5.5	4%
Knowledge About Print	895	15	10%
Writing Activities	530	9	6%
Oral Language Activities	820	14	9%
Content-Area Literacy	410	7	4%
All Literacy Combined	3,795	63	42%

kindergartens. The literacy activities include six categories each with several activities listed. These teacher-initiated activities or categories with their subcategories included the following:

Storybook reading activities: telling stories, reading stories to children, teacher modeling of storytelling with the use of props, reading poetry, visiting the library, children reading independently, and reading magazines.

Activities related to knowledge about print: letter recognition, whole-word recognition, word families, sound-symbol relations, directionality, chanting rhymes, creating rhymes, color identification, and shape identification.

Comprehension strategies: prestory discussion, poststory discussion, discussion about story structure and sequencing, literal activities, story retelling by children, and following directions.

Writing activities: writing stories, making books, dictating stories to the teacher, taking dictation from the teacher, teacher writing morning message, teacher writing experience charts, journal writing, writing about pictures, writing letters to others, and collecting Very-own words. (Very-own words are those that children wish to have and learn. The teacher or child writes the word on a 3 × 5 card, which is placed in a storage container, such as a plastic bag. The child practices the words, copies them, and uses them in sentences. The words are usually ones that have a special meaning for the child.)

Oral language activities: vocabulary development, sharing time or show and tell, discussions related to thematic units, calendar, the weather, and stones.

Literacy integrated into content areas: literacy occurred in activities involving cooking, social studies, science, play, music, art, and math, and in free-choice center time.

Free-choice center time was counted because children engaged in different types of self-initiated reading, writing, and oral language during this period.

Comparison of Time Spent in Literacy Activities and in Other Types of Activities

Tables 3 and 4 indicate which activities were observed in each of the 10 classrooms with the number of different types of activities recorded for each teacher's room totaled. The teachers in whole-day and half-day programs did activities in all of the six major categories that emerged. The teachers in the whole-day programs used an average of 24.8 different types of literacy activities within the major categories, and the teachers in the half-day kindergartens used an average of 19.6 activities.

Tables 3 and 4 also present the amount of time spent on teacher-initiated activities in the six categories of literacy recorded in the five whole-day and five half-day programs, with 12 observations per room. A total of 7,745 minutes was spent on teacher-initiated literacy

31

Table 3
Comparison of Total Time, Average Time, and Percentage of Instructional Time Spent in Literacy Activities for Whole-Day Kindergartens

	Total Time (in Minutes)	Average Time (in Minutes)	Percentage of Instructional Time
Storybook Activities:	2,365	34.4	16%
Tells stories	460		
Reads to children	1,290		
Tells prop stories	325		
Reads poetry	125		
Visits library	40		
Children read independently	0		
Magazines	125		
Comprehension Strategies:	660	11	4%
Prestory discussion	155		
Poststory discussion	340		
Story structure sequencing	70		
Literal activities	30		
Retelling	20		
Following directions	45		
Knowledge About Print:	1,875	31	12%
Letter recognition	1,015		
Word recognition	240		
Word families	60		
Sound-symbol relations	100		
Rhyme chanting	125		
Directionality	30		
Creating rhymes	105		
Colors (Reading readiness)	0		
Shapes (Reading readiness)	200		
Writing Activities:	955	16	6%
Very-own words	50		
Writing stories	0		
Making books	255		
Dictation to teacher	70		

(continued)

Table 3
Comparison of Total Time, Average Time, and
Percentage of Instructional Time Spent in Literacy
Activities for Whole-Day Kindergartens (continued)

Dictation from teacher	0		
Writes morning message	100		
Writes experience chart	60		
Journal writing	285		
Writes about picture	105		
Writes letter	30		
Oral Language Activities:	1,060	18	7%
Vocabulary development	135		
Sharing time (show and tell)	390		
Content-area discussion	140		
Calendar/weather	395		
Content-Area Literacy:	830	14	5%
Cooking	25		
Social studies	20		
Science	180		
Play	60		
Music	240		
Art	60		
Math	245		
All Literacy	7,745	129	51%

activities in the whole-day kindergartens over the 12 observations, which means on a typical day in a whole-day classroom, the average amount of teacher-initiated literacy activity was 129 minutes. For the five half-day kindergartens, the total time spent on teacher-initiated literacy activities was 3,795 minutes over the 12 observations. Therefore, the average amount of time spent on these activities on a typical day in a half-day classroom was 63 minutes.

To make a reasonable comparison between the half-day and whole-day settings, the percentage of the instructional time spent on literacy was calculated. For this study, instructional time was defined as time spent on all instructional activities that occurred in whole-day and half-day kindergartens. This excluded time devoted to lunch, recess,

Table 4
Comparison of Total Time, Average Time, and
Percentage of Instructional Time Spent in Literacy
Activities for Half-Day Kindergartens

	Total Time (in Minutes)	Average Time (in Minutes)	Percentage of Instructional Time
Storybook Activities:	810	13.5	9%
Tells stories	65		
Reads to children	670		
Tells prop stories	20		
Reads poetry	10		
Visits library	0		
Children read independently	45		
Magazines	0		
Comprehension Strategies:	330	5.5	4%
Prestory discussion	110		
Poststory discussion	160		
Story structure sequencing	20		
Literal activities	20		
Retelling	20		
Following directions	0		
Knowledge About Print:	895	15	10%
Letter recognition	550		
Word recognition	100		
Word families	10		
Sound-symbol relations	0		
Rhyme chanting	80		
Directionality	50		
Creating rhymes	50		
Colors (Reading readiness)	10		
Shapes (Reading readiness)	45		
Writing Activities:	530	9	6%
Very-own words	0		
Writing stories	0		
Making books	115		
Dictation to teacher	0		

(continued)

Table 4
**Comparison of Total Time, Average Time, and
Percentage of Instructional Time Spent in Literacy
Activities for Half-Day Kindergartens (continued)**

Dictation from teacher	5		
Writes morning message	85		
Writes experience chart	40		
Journal writing	185		
Writes about picture	75		
Writes letter	25		
Oral Language Activities:	820	14	9%
Vocabulary development	95		
Sharing time (show and tell)	150		
Content-area discussion	155		
Calendar/weather	420		
Content-Area Literacy:	410	7	4%
Cooking	0		
Social studies	0		
Science	50		
Play	0		
Music	255		
Art	65		
Math	40		
All Literacy	3,795	63	42%

following lunch, and rest. Therefore, the amount of instructional time in whole-day classrooms was 255 minutes per day. For half-day classrooms, it was 150 minutes. The percentage of instructional time spent on teacher-initiated literacy activities for whole-day kindergartens was 51% (129 minutes/255 minutes $\times$ 100%). For the half-day kindergartens, the percentage of instructional time spent in teacher-initiated literacy activities was 42% (63 minutes/150 minutes $\times$ 100%).

A look at the six major categories of literacy activities recorded indicates that in all cases the whole-day kindergartners spent more time engaged in literacy activities than did the students in the half-day program. The major category of *Storybook Activities* accounted for the largest amount of time. A total of 2,365 minutes was recorded as spent on storybook activities in the five whole-day kindergartens over the 12 observations. In the half-day program there was a total of 810 minutes over the 12 observations. On a typical day in a whole-day classroom there was an average of 39.4 minutes of storybook activities observed, and in a half-day classroom, an average of 13.5 minutes of storybook activities. The percentage of instructional time spent on storybook activities in the whole-day kindergartens was 16% (39.4 minutes/255 minutes $\times$ 100%). In the half-day programs it was 9% (13.5 minutes/150 minutes $\times$ 100%).

In the major category of *Comprehension Strategies* a total of 660 minutes was spent in the whole-day kindergartens, resulting in an average of 11 minutes for a class on a typical day. In the five half-day programs the total was 330 minutes for an average of 5.5 minutes spent on comprehension activities on a typical day. This represents 4% of the instructional time in both whole-day and half-day programs.

In the major category of *Knowledge About Print*, 1,875 minutes were spent in the 12 whole-day sessions for an average of 31 minutes. In the half-day program 895 minutes were spent for an average of 15 minutes. This represented 12% of the instructional time in the whole-day programs and 10% of the instructional time in the half-day programs.

Writing Activities accounted for 955 minutes over the 12 observations in the 5 whole-day kindergartens for an average of 16 minutes. In the half-day programs 530 minutes were spent on writing in the 12 sessions observed, for an average of 9 minutes per session. Writing activities represented 6% of the instructional time in both half-day and whole-day programs.

In the *Oral Language* category, 1,060 minutes were spent in the whole-day program, for an average of 18 minutes per session. This represented 7% of the instructional time. In the half-day program 820 minutes over 12 sessions were recorded for an average of 14 minutes per session, representing 9% of the instructional time.

The last category to emerge was *Content-Area Literacy*. There were 830 minutes recorded in which literacy activity occurred for an average of 14 minutes in the whole-day programs, representing 5% of the instructional time. In the half-day programs 410 minutes were spent over the 12 sessions for an average of 7 minutes. This represented 4% of the instructional time.

Organizational Structures Used in Whole-Day and Half-Day Programs During Literacy Instruction

As we observed literacy activities that took place and the amount of time spent in the activities in the whole-day and half-day kindergartens, we also recorded whether the literacy activities were in whole-group, small-group, or one-on-one settings. We observed whether learning settings were teacher directed or student initiated. Table 5 presents the amount of time the whole-day and half-day kindergarten teachers organized their classes in whole-group, small-group, and one-on-one settings.

In the whole-day kindergarten 6,465 minutes were recorded in whole-group literacy instruction. This came to an average of 108 minutes per classroom and represented 83% of the time spent on literacy activities. In the half-day programs, 3,255 minutes were spent in whole-group instruction for an average of 54 minutes, which represents 85% of literacy instruction. Small-group settings occurred less frequently for a total of 1,060 minutes in whole-day programs, an av-

Table 5
Comparison of Organizational Structures Observed in Whole-Day and Half-Day Kindergartens

	Total Time (in Minutes)	Average Time (in Minutes)	Percentage of Literacy Time
Whole-Day			
Literacy	7,745	129	
Whole group	6,465	108	83%
Small group (centers)	1,060	18	13%
One-on-one	370	6	4%
Half-Day			
Literacy	3,795	63	
Whole group	3,255	54	85%
Small group (centers)	325	5.5	8%
One-on-one	305	5	7%

erage of 18 minutes or 13% of literacy instruction time. In the half-day programs 325 minutes were spent in small-group instruction for an average of 5.5 minutes or 8% of literacy instruction. One-on-one settings between teacher and student were the least frequent with 370 minutes recorded in whole-day classes for an average of 6 minutes or 4% of literacy time. In the half-day programs 305 minutes were spent in one-on-one settings for an average of 5 minutes or 7% of literacy time.

The percentages presented in Table 5 are related to the organizational structures used by the teachers and are not linked to the total instructional time. Rather, they indicate the percentage of literacy time spent in a given structural format. Instruction using these formats was all teacher initiated. Instruction that allowed for student-initiated activities occurred during free-choice center time.

Student-Initiated Activities in Free-Choice Center Time

During center time children engaged in many activities, some of which involved a great deal of literacy. Very often, children were engaged in social situations where they had the opportunity to interact with one another, make their own choices about what they would do, collaborate in pairs or small groups, and practice literacy skills they had learned.

Table 6 presents the amount of time spent in free-choice center time. Because children were involved with literacy during free-choice time, we felt that these data were important to collect. We decided to try to determine the types and number of literacy activities in which they participated. Because we did not have the resources to watch every child in the different centers over the 12 observations, we randomly selected two half-day and two whole-day kindergartens from among those with which we were working. Three girls and three boys were then selected randomly from each classroom and the types of literacy activities in which they engaged during free-choice time were observed and recorded. One child in the half-day and one in the whole-day transferred out of the program after a few observations; therefore we had data for 11 children in both groups. We also looked at the number and types of activities other than literacy that these children selected to participate in during free-choice center time.

The observations revealed that during free-choice center time children did take part in self-initiated literacy activities. The children

Table 6
Comparison of Free-Choice Center Time in Whole-Day
and Half-Day Kindergartens

	Total Time (in Minutes)	Average Time (in Minutes)	Percentage of Instructional Time
Whole-Day	1,500	25	10%
Half-Day	1,130	19	13%

participated in a total of 64 literacy activities in the whole-day program and 51 other free-choice center activities during the 12 observations. In the half-day programs there were 42 literacy activities recorded and 56 other activities selected in the center areas. The total number of different literacy activities recorded for whole-day kindergartens was 27, and 19 were recorded for half-day.

The data show that children in whole-day kindergarten engaged in literacy activities more than children in the half-day programs and selected a wider variety of literacy activities in which to participate. In the whole-day kindergarten, of the 11 children being observed there were 11 absences during the 12 days of observations and 9 absences in the half-day program. In the half-day program one child was directed to the timeout chair three times during observations, and in the half-day program there were four timeouts.

The literacy activities observed took place in the art center, math center, literacy center, dramatic play, and block areas. The 11 children in the whole-day program were observed participating in the following types of literacy activities:

Reading: conventional and emergent oral reading of books, magazines, and newspapers alone and with others.

Print-awareness activities: using alphabet board games, tracing cardboard letters, using the computer for letter identification games, and matching words to pictures.

Listening: use of headsets with taped stories to listen to books.

Writing: emergent and conventional writing for creating books, writing on the blackboard, writing greeting cards, writing letters, journal writing, copying charts, dictating stories to the teacher, writing stories, and writing stories on the computer.

Demonstration of comprehension through story retelling: use of puppets to retell a story, felt characters and a felt board to retell a story, a roll story box to retell a story, and doing a chalk talk to retell a story (drawing the story as it is told).

Dramatic play and literacy: reading and writing activities in a dramatic-play setting created either by the teacher or themselves (pretending to be a waitress in the dramatic-play area that was set up to be a restaurant or writing patient charts for toy animals when the dramatic-play area was designed like a veterinarian's office).

Activities participated in other than literacy: We also recorded the activities other than literacy activities in which the children participated. Children were observed participating in 51 other activities in the half-day program and 56 in the whole-day program with the same activities taking place in both programs. Activities include the following:

<u>Art activities</u>: making play dough, creating objects with play dough, easel painting, coloring pictures on blackline masters, creating original pictures, and making collages.

<u>Games</u>: use of computer games, puzzles, board games, and other toys.

<u>Block play</u>: creating block structures and role playing with the structures.

<u>Imaginative play</u>: role playing in the dramatic-play kitchen area, at the water play table, and the sand or rice table.

<u>Math center</u>: use of the computer for math games, use of geometric shapes, a balance scale, and magnetic numbers on a magnetic board.

In the half-day program children participated in some of the same self-initiated literacy activities as did the whole-day children including reading, print-awareness activities, listening, and writing. There were no recorded observations, however, in the areas of demonstrating comprehension through story retellings or reading and writing in dramatic-play settings. Kindergartners in whole-day and half-day programs worked on literacy activities in both groups and alone, collaborated on projects, and sometimes tutored one another.

We felt this free-choice center data was particularly important because when literacy activities did occur in this setting they were student initiated, and in a social situation where children had the opportunity to interact with one another, select what they wanted to participate in, collaborate, and practice skills learned.

Literacy Materials Used in Whole-Day and Half-Day Kindergartens

Because literacy materials provides the means for literacy activities, observers noted the types of materials used by teachers and children in the whole-day and half-day kindergartens. The list included basal readers, Big Books, book-binding materials, calendars, chalkboard, chalk, children's literature, the computer, costumes for role playing stories, crayons, environmental print, experience charts, felt boards with felt story characters, felt-tipped pens, headsets with taped stories, index cards for students' own words, journals, magazines, overhead projector, pens, pencils, poetry, posters, puppets, props for storytelling, roll stories, story-writing paper, teacher-made literacy materials (skill games), published literacy manipulatives for skill development, teacher manuals, video stories, and worksheets. The whole-day kindergartens used the 32 materials listed here. The half-day kindergartens used only some of these materials. Those not used or not present in the half-day rooms were costumes for role playing, headsets and taped stories, props for storytelling, environmental print, index cards for students' own words, video stories, magazines, and an overhead projector.

Teacher and Child Interviews

In addition to our observational data we interviewed teachers and children to find out the positive and negative aspects of whole-day and half-day kindergarten. The five whole-day and five half-day teachers were interviewed individually. The results of our interviews are recorded on the following pages.

Half-Day Teachers' Responses to Questionnaire

1. What do you think are the benefits to teaching half-day kindergarten?
   - Activities done in the morning session that do not go well can be modified in the afternoon class.
   - The amount of time in the school day seems appropriate for children this age; they don't seem to get tired.
2. What don't you like about a half-day kindergarten program?
   - There isn't enough time to get all the necessary activities into the school day.
   - There isn't enough time to give each child adequate attention.
3. About how much time in your day do you spend on literacy instruction?
   - All teachers answered about one hour.
4. Describe the types of literacy activities you do frequently in your classroom.
   - Whole group: stories, questions, choral reading, and morning message.
   - Small group: reading groups, journal writing, and assigned center activities such as listening to stories on headsets.
   - Center work: Students work individually and cooperatively in small groups in centers doing literacy activities.
5. What do you think would be advantageous about whole-day kindergarten?
   - There would be more time to get to know children.
   - There would be more time to do activities in depth.
   - There would be more time for additional literacy activities.
   - There would be more time for skill development.
   - There would be time for children to socialize, play, and explore.
   - It would provide a setting that wouldn't be rushed.
   - It allows time to plan for activities that are interesting and fun.
6. What do you think are the disadvantages of whole-day kindergarten?
   - It is a long day for children.
7. How much time do you think you would spend on literacy in a whole-day kindergarten program?
   - The average response was 2 to 3 hours.

8. Do you think your literacy instruction would be different in whole-day than in half-day kindergarten?
- I would spend larger blocks of time on activities than I do now.
- I could do more activities than I do now.
- I would have more time for children to work in centers that allow them to participate in literacy activities on their own.

9. Do you believe students will score better on literacy achievement in whole-day kindergarten?
- Four responded yes, one responded no.

10. If you had your choice would you rather teach in a whole-day or half-day kindergarten program?
- All five teachers responded they would prefer to teach in a whole-day program.

Whole-Day Teachers' Responses to Questionnaire

1. What do you think are the benefits to teaching half-day kindergarten?
- You can improve what you do in the morning in the afternoon.
- I don't think there are any.

2. What don't you like about a half-day kindergarten program?
- There isn't enough time to cover materials.
- There isn't enough time to plan activities that are fun.
- Since you have two classes of children you have two sets of paper work to do.

3. About how much time in your day did you spend on literacy instruction when you taught half-day kindergarten?
- All responded about 1 hour.

4. Describe the types of literacy activities you did when you taught half-day programs.
- Whole-group storybook reading.
- Small-group reading instruction.
- Dictation of stories by children to the teacher.
- Journal writing.
- Literacy activities embedded into thematic instruction.

5. Describe the nature of the literacy activities in your whole-day program.
- All of the same activities are done in whole-day as in half-day, however there are larger blocks of time to do them in.
- You can do more literacy activities.

- You can allot more time at the literacy center where children engage in literacy with other children and get to choose what they would like to do.

6. What do you think would be advantageous about whole-day kindergarten?
- I get to know the children and their needs better.
- I can balance my school day with skills development and opportunities for exploring through art, music, and play—both indoors and outdoors.
- The school day isn't rushed.
- I can do more activities in depth.

7. What do you think are the disadvantages of whole-day kindergarten?
- Since we don't have a bathroom in the room with the whole-day program this becomes a problem.
- Sometimes the day seems long for some children.

8. How much time do you spend on literacy in a whole-day kindergarten program?
- 2 to 3 hours.

9. Do you think your literacy instruction in your whole-day class is different than when you taught half-day kindergarten?
- I spend larger blocks of time on activities than I could in half-day.
- I do more activities.
- I have more time for children to work in centers, allowing them to participate in self-initiated literacy activities.
- I get to work in small groups with children more often and on a one-to-one basis.
- We aren't rushed.

10. Do you believe students will score better on literacy achievement in whole-day kindergarten?
- Three responded yes.
- Two said, "I don't know, I'm not sure if more school will result in higher scores."

11. If you had your choice would you rather teach in a whole-day or half-day kindergarten program?
- All five teachers responded they would prefer to teach in a whole-day program. They included the following reasons:
- Half-day is too rushed.

- You can accomplish more in whole-day.
- You can use more developmentally appropriate teaching strategies because you have the time for large blocks for learning and meeting individual needs.

12. Do you feel it is better for children to attend whole-day rather than half-day?
- Yes, I think children learn more.
- I think they can have more fun.
- Whole-day programs allow for easy adjustment to first grade.
- For some children a shorter day might be better.
- Only if the program is based on developmentally appropriate practice. Otherwise, the extra time won't mean anything.

Child Interviews Concerning Whole-Day and Half-Day Kindergarten

We interviewed children to see if there were any trends about their feelings toward school when attending whole-day and half-day kindergarten. These were the same children who were selected randomly at the beginning of the study to test for achievement. We recorded interview data for 30 whole-day and 30 half-day students.

When asked if they got tired in school, 12 children in the half-day kindergartens said yes and 18 said no. In the whole-day program 17 children said yes and 13 said no.

When asked when they got tired during the school day, whole-day students said: after lunch, when it is time to go home, early in the morning, at rest time, after school, when doing work, before lunch, and at play time. Children in the half-day program had very similar responses; they said: when it is time to go home, early in the morning, at math, when it is clean up time, and any time.

When asked if they thought the school day was too long, 16 children in the whole-day program said yes and 14 said no; 10 children in the half-day program said yes and 20 said no. The answers in response to the question "Why do you think the school day is too long?" were exactly the same for whole-day and half-day children. They responded as follows: I get tired, I get bored, it isn't fun, and it is a lot of work.

When asked if school should be longer, 8 children in the whole-day program said yes and 22 said no. Eighteen children in the half-day program said school should be longer and 12 said it should not. When those who thought that school should be longer were asked why, they responded as follows:

- I have nothing to do at home.
- We do good things at school.
- We have fun.
- It makes me work and learn more.
- I can get to play with my friends more.

Anecdotal Observations

In addition to observing the types of literacy activities that occurred and the number of minutes spent on literacy in half-day and whole-day kindergartens, we also observed children's general impressions of what it felt like to be in both types of kindergarten programs. After observing literacy activities and interviewing teachers and children, we wanted a more holistic view to confirm the findings thus far or shed a different light on the data collected. The same two individuals observed children in every whole-day and half-day kindergarten in the investigation. In addition, each of the researchers observing in whole-day programs on a regular basis observed in a half-day program once, and vice versa. The researchers observed the physical settings of the classroom and recorded the general schedule of the school day and activities that occurred. More specifically they observed the teacher and children, looking for the atmosphere that was present to try to make some generalizations about whole-day and half-day programs from several different perspectives. We had a total of 22 reports with data of this type to code for trends. Examples of anecdotal records for the seven different types of literacy activities observed are included in Appendix C.

The physical environments varied from one classroom to the next, but generally the length of the school day did not seem to greatly affect the physical setting of the kindergartens. A few observers reported the presence of more centers that were better defined and had more equipment in them in the whole-day settings. More time was spent in whole-day programs with children using centers in a structured manner doing teacher-assigned activities and using them in a more informal way with student-initiated activities. Because more time was spent in centers, teachers probably had to supply them with adequate materials for children's use, which may be why these centers were better equipped.

The schedules for the school day in both whole-day and half-day programs had many things in common. Very similar activities occurred. It was observed that more activities could be carried out in the whole-day classrooms and that larger blocks of time were set aside for different experiences in the whole-day programs. The types of developmentally appropriate practices researchers and teachers would hope to see were present in both whole-day and half-day programs such as the use of thematic instruction integrated throughout the school day; use of experience charts, morning messages, and journal writing; use of computers related to literacy; varied storybook reading experiences; and variety in the structural organization of classroom instruction such as whole-group, small-group, and one-on-one settings.

The observations of whole-day and half-day programs revealed and supported information already found in our literature review (see Chapter 1), in the observations of the kindergartens for time spent on literacy activities, and in the interviews with teachers and children. This information suggests that whole-day kindergartens

- are more relaxed, because the day moves at a comfortable pace for teachers and students;
- afford the opportunity for a variety of educational experiences;
- have more time to be concerned about the physical, social, emotional, and intellectual development of the child;
- allow for more in-depth development of concepts due to large blocks of time for learning experiences;
- allow for dealing with more skill development;
- enable children to have more opportunities for events such as field trips and for taking part in special school activities such as assemblies;
- afford the teacher the opportunity to get to know the individual needs, strengths, and interests of children and to pursue those needs and interests; and
- provide more time to meet individual needs by working with classroom teachers and special resource teachers.

However, along with these good points there were some problems. As the day progressed, some children seemed tired.

Half-day programs had their advantages and disadvantages. The major advantage stated was that the half-day program seemed to allow an appropriate amount of time for children of this age to be in school. A disadvantage of the half-day program is that it can cause a midday disruption for students who need additional day care.

In general, however, the comparative reports on the general atmosphere of the whole-day versus the half-day programs did not differ. The major complaint of the half-day programs was that the atmosphere was rushed. Teachers can deal with this problem by eliminating some activities from each day and deal with fewer activities over longer blocks of learning time, which seems to be preferable.

The major complaint with the whole-day programs was the length of the school day. A way to remedy this problem is to make the whole-day program a bit shorter than the regular school day or, as some districts already do, begin the school year with a shorter day and increase the length of the day slowly in the first few months of school. Careful selection of activity scheduling can help with attention span. The general consensus from the observers was that whole-day seemed preferable when all of the advantages and disadvantages were weighed.

The argument for the length of the day being too long for kindergarten-age children made by the observers and some teachers seems difficult to support. Many children have attended day care prior to kindergarten and have been in school not only from the typical 9 a.m. to 3 p.m. school day, but from 7 a.m. until 6 p.m., and many children who attend half-day programs are sent to a day care for the remainder of the day when their parents work. It may be more developmentally appropriate to stay in the same place rather than have to move and make an adjustment to an entirely new environment with new children and new teachers, but further research needs to determine if this is true.

In this chapter we have presented the results of both the quantitative and qualitative data we collected. There has been no attempt to analyze or discuss what these results mean. In Chapter 4 we will summarize the results and discuss implications for classroom practice and further research on the topic.

Discussion of Results: Implications of the Data Analysis for Classroom Practice

Discussion of the Results From Literacy Achievement Data

The results from the literacy achievement data indicate that the children in the whole-day kindergarten scored significantly better on all the tests administered than the children in the half-day program. The tests referred to were: Comprehension, Story Retelling, Writing, Story Reenactment, Teacher Rating of Reading Ability, Teacher Rating of Reading Interest, and the Kindergarten Inventory. It has been argued however, that it is not the quantity of the program that counts but the quality. As mentioned in Chapter 1, according to the NAEYC, the most important element in early childhood programming is not the time spent in the classroom, but the developmentally appropriate nature of the program. The NAEYC suggests a longer day would be better than one that is shorter only in the instance of a quality program. The distinction is an important one because the afternoon portion of a whole-day program could consist of time spent poorly.

The results of this investigation support the views of the NAEYC. Because the kindergarten curriculum designed by the administrators and teachers in the district where the study took place was based on developmentally appropriate practices, there was concern for the social, emotional, physical, and intellectual growth of the child. Literacy objectives followed an emergent literacy perspective and the integrated language arts approach to literacy instruction. With the type of kindergarten program described in the previous two sentences being implemented in whole-day and half-day settings, longer *was* demonstrated to be better.

Discussion of the Results From the Observational Data

The observational data help support the results of the literacy achievement data. Although the whole-day and half-day teachers initiated literacy activities in the same major categories of Storybook Reading, Knowledge About Print, Comprehension Strategies, Writing Activities, Oral Language Activities, and Literacy Integrated Into Content Areas, because there was more time in the school day, the whole-day programs spent more time engaged in these experiences. The whole-day programs also used additional activities modeled and scaffolded for children under the major categories, probably because they had the additional time.

Whole-day programs allowed more variety in the organizational management within the literacy program and teachers in the whole-day program had the opportunity to do more whole-group, small-group, and one-on-one instruction. In these one-on-one settings and in small groups, children receive rich scaffolding experiences from teachers that they can transfer into other settings at another time. However, the amount of time spent in whole-group settings was far more than time devoted to small-group and one-on-one instruction. Teachers in both types of kindergartens need to be more aware of how they are organizing for instruction and, where appropriate, reorganize the balance of time in the different structures. More time could be devoted to small-group and one-on-one instruction and less in the whole-group setting.

In addition, as mentioned in the previous chapter, there was more time in the all-day programs for student-initiated free-choice center time. Students spent more time in this social setting where they had choices of literacy activities to participate in. They also selected many more different types of activities.

It is possible that the additional time spent on literacy in the whole-day kindergartens motivated children to try more and do more literacy during free-choice center time when they could select activities. The half-day children did not have the benefit of as much exposure to as many of these activities and did not have as much attention given to them in small-group and one-on-one situations.

It is interesting to note that although more time was spent on literacy in all areas in the whole-day programs, the proportion of instructional time devoted to literacy was about the same in all categories for the whole-day and half-day classrooms. This suggests that the half-day programs we observed were doing as good a job as possible in the limited time they had, and that whole-day programs were using their additional time to its best advantage with carefully selected literacy activities.

Summary of Teacher Interview Responses

Teacher interview responses in half-day and whole-day programs were similar. The general consensus was that half-day kindergarten is too short to accomplish in-depth goals because it is rushed and because it is difficult in half-day settings to get to know the needs of all the children.

Interviews from teachers generally were in favor of whole-day programs with some reservations. According to the teachers, the advantages to the longer day are longer blocks of time for more in-depth learning, getting to know students better to attend to their individual needs, the ability to do more activities, and the ability to keep the developmentally appropriate flavor to their kindergartens with time for play, exploration, and socialization. The main disadvantage was concern that the length of the day was sometimes too long for the attention span of some of the children. The main advantage mentioned for the half-day program was the appropriate length of the school day for kindergarten children.

Summary of Child Interviews

Responses to the child interview questions do indicate that more children in whole-day programs said they get tired during the school day than those in half-day programs. More of them also suggested that the school day is too long. Fewer whole-day children said they would like for the school day to be longer. It would be interesting to ask first- and second-grade children these same questions to determine their attitudes toward the length of their school day. This could indicate that the age of the kindergarten child is a definite factor in determining attitude toward the length of the school day, or it could indicate that when the school day goes past the lunch hour older children find they get tired as well.

When we asked if the school day should be longer, more half-day than whole-day children responded yes. It is interesting that 18 of the 30 half-day children said that school should be longer; but the answers the children gave as to why school should be longer are even more interesting and worth paying attention to: I have nothing to do at home, we do good things at school, we have fun at school, it makes me work and learn, and I can play with my friends. These reasons are probably exactly why we would propose that children stay in school longer.

Discussion of Anecdotal Observations

The research assistants who observed both whole-day and half-day programs seemed to favor whole-day for the many reasons that have already been stated. None of these observers discussed the length of the school day as an issue. Observers described the atmosphere in the classrooms as being just as appropriate in whole-day settings as in half-day, and not one discussed restlessness on the part of the children or a lack of attention span where nothing productive could occur. Mostly the observers reported on the atmosphere of the classroom based on the manner in which teachers acted toward children.

A particular theme became clear in the observation reports of the half-day and whole-day programs aside from the physical environments, daily schedules, literacy activities, and other activities carried out. As one observer wrote,

> The atmosphere in the classrooms I observed were very different, and I do not think it is a matter of the amount of time that the teachers have, but the style of teaching that they employ. It is how they speak to children, the positive and constructive reinforcement they offer, the enthusiasm and sense of humor they bring to their teaching, the respect they have for children, and the respect that they instill in the children for each other.

Through multiple reports of classroom observations in all half-day and whole-day rooms the same theme kept occurring to describe good teaching aside from the effects, advantages, or disadvantages of whole-day and half-day programs. Exemplary classrooms had teachers who possessed certain characteristics that have an effect on the quality of a classroom setting. The following characteristics were observed repeatedly:

- The classroom has an atmosphere that is enjoyable, because the teacher is fun to be with and has a definite sense of humor.
- The teacher provides varied activities.
- Children are encouraged to express themselves freely.
- The teacher has patience to offer help when needed.
- When a teacher loves his or her job, it is clear to the children.
- The classroom provides a happy, comfortable, relaxed atmosphere because the teacher seems happy, comfortable, and relaxed as a teacher.
- The teacher is warm, caring, loving, and friendly.
- The teacher shows a strong interest in each and every child and his or her individual needs.
- The teacher encourages children to take risks.
- The teacher offers positive and constructive feedback and discipline with dignity.
- The class is never affected by the discipline of one student.
- The teacher takes pride in the children's work.
- The class is organized, with a predictable routine and a predictable teacher, and children know what is expected of them.
- Student independence is fostered.
- The teacher creates a pleasant, nurturing, and emotionally healthy atmosphere.
- The teacher speaks in a pleasant tone and rarely raises his or her voice.
- The teacher smiles often.
- There is a social atmosphere in the classroom.

Although the characteristics that made for exemplary teaching atmospheres was not a question for this particular investigation, it seemed worthwhile to report. This would be an important area for discussion in future research.

Implications for Classroom Practice

It appears from this investigation that children would benefit from a longer school day, provided that a kindergarten program is using what is considered to be a developmentally appropriate practice.

We cannot ignore the demographics of families today as an important issue in determining the whole-day or half-day issue. Many mothers of kindergarten-age children work. If the children are not in a whole-day kindergarten, they will be placed into an afternoon program, into another morning program, or with someone to care for them. The quality of the program or the individual in charge may not live up to the standards set for kindergarten classrooms. Public schools therefore need to take a leading role in designing quality whole-day programs.

With appropriate planning the problems of the length of the school day can be overcome with a shorter day at the beginning of the school year that increases over time. It also can be helped with careful scheduling of appropriate activities at different times during the school day.

As a result of the investigation and the observations in the classroom it became apparent that the length of the school day did have an effect on literacy achievement and the types of activities for which teachers had time.

Implications for Research

Although the data from this study seem to favor whole-day kindergarten there is still more research to be done. Most of the existing research is outdated and has not been designed with ample scientific rigor to make definitive decisions. Issues that need to be pursued are parents' attitudes toward the length of the school day, the effect of the school day on different populations, longitudinal studies to examine effect over time, and additional issues concerning academic achievement in areas other than literacy. Certainly we need to investigate the emotional and social benefits to either whole-day or half-day programs.

This study also indicates that the type of activities teachers prepared as well as the organization and management of the school day are more important than its length. In the following chapters we discuss frameworks for the literacy curriculum and plans for organizing whole-day and half-day kindergarten programs. This information was drawn from perspectives on early literacy and developmentally appropriate programming for kindergarten classrooms that exist in the research literature and from the best practices, organization, and management of activities we observed in the classrooms in our research. Before looking at specific ways to improve instruction in both half-day and whole-day kindergarten classrooms, we will look at the literature on emergent literacy.

CHAPTER 5

Emergent Literacy Perspectives: Research to Practice

Five-year-old Darren ran up to the teacher to read a story he had written for his pen pal. On his page was an illustration and above the drawing were letter-like forms and some real letters (see Figure 1).

Darren's story demonstrates his knowledge of writing and reading. Even though his writing is not yet conventional, he knows the difference between print and pictures and the functions of each. He has a sense of what writing looks like and that it goes from left to right on the page. Finally, he obviously recognizes that illustrations can be related to the print found in books.

Research in early literacy identifies Darren's accomplishments as emergent literacy behavior. Although the literacy skills and knowledge he demonstrates may seem unconventional to an adult, his performance is to be rewarded and encouraged. The task he has taken on is a functional one: sending a story to his pen pal. He has a real-life reason for writing and writes in social context, sharing his work with the teacher and with a friend. Darren is actively involved in a literacy experience.

This example illustrates some of the insights about early literacy development discovered through our research and how we have come to understand them. Attempting to identify how literacy is acquired in early childhood, researchers observe children engaged in literacy activities, approaching their task from the child's perspective. We also know that children need to see adults model literacy activities for them and guide them with some direct instruction to help foster development.

Figure 1
Darren's Story

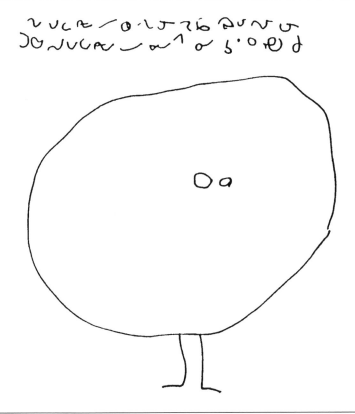

From Lesley M. Morrow, *Literacy Development in the Early Years: Helping Children Read and Write* (3rd Edition). Copyright 1997 by Allyn & Bacon. Reprinted by permission.

Defining Emergent Literacy

The term "emergent literacy" was first used by Clay (1966). The concept assumes that children acquire some knowledge about language, reading, and writing before coming to school. Literacy development begins early and continues throughout life, and there is a dynamic relation among the communication skills. Each skill influences the others in the course of development that occurs in the everyday contexts of home and community. Clay defined emergent literacy as only those behaviors demonstrated by children that were not yet conventional; when a child began to read and write in a manner similar to that of an adult, he or she no longer was considered to be an emergent reader and writer. However, children are always emerging in their reading and writing. We must acknowledge their individual accomplishments and reward their growth as they progress.

Young children possess certain literacy skills, though the skills are neither fully developed nor conventional as we recognize mature reading and writing (Teale, 1986). Emergent literacy acknowledges that a child is involved in legitimate literacy behavior when he or she narrates a familiar storybook while looking at the pictures and occasionally at the print. Although the reading is not conventional, the child gives the impression of reading through tone of voice, attention to pages and illustrations, and following a left-to-right progression across pages (Sulzby, 1985).

Emergent literacy approaches are different from reading-readiness approaches. Reading-readiness activities are seen as precursors to reading, and the activities that take place under this rubric are typically not reading or writing of any type. Rather, some educators believe their mastery to be necessary before formal reading can begin. Reading readiness, for instance, suggests systematically teaching a set of prescribed skills such as the learning of letters and sounds with the assumption that all children are at fairly similar levels of development when they come to kindergarten and need these skills before attempting to read and write (Teale & Sulzby, 1986).

Teale (1982) views the development of early literacy as the result of children's involvement in reading activities mediated by more literate others. The social interaction in these activities makes them very significant to a child's development. Not only do interactive literacy events teach children the societal function and conventions of reading, they also link reading with enjoyment and satisfaction and thus increase children's desire to engage in literacy activities. Teale's emphasis on the social aspects of reading development reflects Vygotsky's (1981) more general theory of intellectual development that all higher mental functions are internalized social relationships.

Skills Involved in Literacy Acquisition

Holdaway (1979) and others define four processes that enable young children to acquire literacy abilities. The first is observation of literacy behaviors—for example, being read to or seeing adults read and write. The second is collaboration, the interaction of another individual with the child, which provides direct guidance, encouragement, motivation, and help. The third is practice, during which the learner attempts alone what has been learned, such as role playing or using invented spelling while writing. This process involves children in experimenting without direction or adult observation, and gives children opportunities to evaluate their own performances, make corrections, and increase skills. In the fourth process, performance, the child shares what has been learned and seeks approval from adults who are supportive and interested (Holdaway, 1986; Smith, 1983).

Educators also have become aware of specific skills that are extremely important to literacy development, specifically the knowledge of phonemic awareness. Concerns about the emergent literacy perspective that fosters a constructivist approach to learning have led to the idea that direct instruction of skills in an organized and systematic fashion is a necessity for many children. The design of a kindergarten program should take into consideration all research providing implications for practice that will enhance literacy development.

We considered this research into early literacy in the staff-development program we worked on with the kindergarten teachers in our research study. We also drew ideas from a statement published by the International Reading Association Committee on Literacy Development in Early Childhood (1990):

1. Literacy development begins early in life, long before children start formal instruction in school.

2. School personnel need to recognize the literacy that children bring with them when they enter school. Early classroom experiences with reading and writing should build on the knowledge and ability that already exist in the child. This is different for each child based on his or her background.

3. Literacy involves concurrent development of oral language, reading, and writing. These language activities are interrelated;

developing ability in one helps development in the others. The integration of the literacy skills into other content areas throughout the school day helps to foster their development.

4. Children's literature is a natural resource for literacy learning. It introduces children into the world of books with material that is interesting and enjoyable. It provides a model of writing and language that is of high quality. Selections to be read to children are chosen based on themes that are being studied in the classroom and topics in which students demonstrate an interest. Literature should be shared in a variety of ways.

5. Children learn best when literacy is based on functional experiences in which there is a specific purpose for reading and writing; likewise reading and writing needs to be based on interest and meaning. The interest and meaning are generated when literacy activities are linked to units or themes being studied in the classroom as well as their own life experiences.

6. Children need opportunities to learn in social settings where they can interact with adults and peers during literacy activities.

7. To meet individual needs direct instruction of skills is necessary to guide and support learning. This instruction should be based on the particular needs of children and should take place in small groups or in one-on-one settings.

8. There should be an organizational plan for skill development and materials used for instruction.

9. Although children's learning about literacy can be described in generalized stages, children can pass through these stages in a variety of ways and at different ages.

10. Adults must serve as models for literacy behavior by demonstrating the use of books and print.

11. The joy of learning needs to be emphasized as a major goal. Early literacy experiences should be designed to develop positive attitudes toward reading and writing. Experiences that are meaningful, interesting, and result in success will produce such attitudes.

In this early literacy perspective, the teaching of reading, writing, oral language, listening, and viewing are taught concurrently in an integrated fashion. Literacy is taught where it is meaningful and functional in coordination with other areas of the curriculum, such as social studies, science, music, art, play, and math. Students are also exposed to a great deal of children's literature. Social interaction is promoted in this approach as children collaborate, consult, and share their work with teachers and peers. There is a scope and sequence of skills and time set aside for some direct instruction, but there is a balance in types of learning settings including spontaneous experiences based on teachable moments. For example, we teach letters and sounds that are used more often first because they are familiar. However, if we are studying animals and we learn about panda bears and polar bears, this is an appropriate time to introduce or reinforce the sound and symbol relation of the letter *P*.

Influential Research in Early Literacy and Its Implications for the Development of a Kindergarten Program

Research investigating early childhood literacy development has brought about changes in classroom practice. Following is a brief review of some of this research. After each section about what research has found there are implications for classroom practice in the design of our kindergarten program.

Oral Language

RESEARCH.   Studies of how children learn oral language reveal that language acquisition is based somewhat on developmental maturity. However, it was concluded that children play an active role in their acquisition of language by constructing language. They imitate the language of adults and create their own when they do not have the conventional words they need to communicate their thoughts. Children's first words are usually functional words, and they are motivated to continue generating language when their attempts are positively reinforced. Children who are constantly exposed to an environment rich in language and who interact with adults using language in a social context develop more facility with oral language than children lacking these opportunities (Bloom, 1972; Brown, 1973; Brown & Bellugi, 1964; Bruner, 1975; Lennenberg, 1967; McNeil, 1970; Menyuk, 1977).

IMPLICATIONS FOR THE KINDERGARTEN PROGRAM.   The implications for this research on classroom practice suggest that we give children the opportunity to use language frequently. They should explore and experiment with language, hear good models of it, and discuss things that are of interest to them. They should play with language in social settings and they need positive reinforcement from adults for their new attempts with their language play. Children will also need explicit guidance with the development of vocabulary, syntax, and pronunciation. Exposure to children's literature will provide a good model of language. The opportunity to talk about books that have been read provides the social setting for language learning. Units of study or themes about topics that interest children provide a forum for learning new words that result from discussing exciting experiences provided by the classroom teacher related to the current topic.

Home Influences

RESEARCH.   Many of the perspectives in early literacy have come from studying homes in which children learned to read without direct instruction before coming to school. Some of what goes on in these homes can be adapted as strategies in school settings.

These homes are rich with materials for reading and writing that are used frequently by children with support and encouragement from adults. Books, magazines, newspapers, pencils, markers, and writing paper abound. Adults in these homes engage regularly in literacy activities and engage in such real-life experiences as writing grocery lists, reading newspapers, and sharing recipes in the kitchen. The activities have meaning and purpose, and they draw from environmental print or print that is part of the everyday surroundings, such as cereal boxes, fast-food logos, and traffic signs. The atmosphere supports literacy involvement and social experiences as adults and children share books they have read, talk with one another, and communicate in writing (Clark, 1976; Durkin, 1966; Morrow, 1983; Teale, 1978). Family members serve as models of involvement in literacy activities. For example, they answer children's questions about books and print and in so doing are providing direct instruction. They read to children frequently and reward them for participating in literacy activities.

IMPLICATIONS FOR THE KINDERGARTEN PROGRAM. We cannot replicate the home environment in the school because the situations are so different, nor would it be appropriate; however, we can adapt elements from the home that seem to foster success in literacy development. We can provide rich literacy environments where children are surrounded by books, writing materials, and the written word. We can make literacy learning more enjoyable by sharing what has been written and read. We can allow the voluntary choice of reading and writing through periods of time in which children have the opportunity to engage in these activities independently. We can provide experiences in which literacy serves a function in schools such as writing thank-you notes to a farmer after visiting his or her farm. An emphasis should be placed on making literacy a pleasant experience through teachers reading to children and children having the opportunity to share their favorite stories with others.

Storybook Reading

RESEARCH. Experience with storybooks is one of the most important ways in which children can experience print. Studies have demonstrated that children who have experiences with books increase their interest in them and in learning to read. Storybook reading enhances background information and sense of story structure and familiarizes children with differences between written and oral language. They learn that printed words have sounds and that print contains meaning. Through listening to well-structured unfamiliar stories, comprehension and language skills develop. Reading to children helps them understand how print functions and how it is used. They learn how to handle a book; become sensitive to left-to-right and front-to-back directionality; recognize that stories have beginnings, middles, and ends; and develop the concept of authorship (Cohen, 1968; Feitelson, Kita, & Goldstein, 1986; Hoffman, 1982; Ninio, 1980; Mason & Au, 1986; Morrow, 1984; Pellegrini & Galda, 1982).

Studies illustrate, however, that it is not just the storybook reading that achieves these benefits, but active participation in the reading event. The social interaction in storybook reading motivates interest, and adults and children cooperatively construct meaning as they pause to comment and respond during the reading. This interaction provides a direct channel of information for the child. The adult helps the child understand by interpreting the written language (Morrow, 1988). Many strategies have been tested to help children acquire skills. Teachers need to implement these strategies, providing direct instruction for the acquisition of comprehension skills when using literature with children.

IMPLICATIONS FOR THE KINDERGARTEN PROGRAM.   Strategies derived from the research on reading stories help children benefit from the storybook reading events by developing concepts about books, print, and story comprehension. Some of these strategies follow.

Use a *guided reading or listening activity* that provides the child with an organizational framework that can be internalized through frequent use and transferred when new material is presented. Guided reading or guided listening is used to help children develop strategies in their literacy development and assess their needs. It involves the following activities:

1. Preparation for listening, with discussions and questions before the story begins. Provide background information or ask children to predict what might happen. Set a goal for listening, such as "Try to remember which part of the story you like best." The objective for every story reading can be different.

2. Read the story with expression and show the illustrations. Pause at natural breaks for children's reactions, comments, or questions. This should be encouraged if the children can chant along with you or read some of the words.

3. Discuss the story after reading. Begin the discussion by focusing on the original objective. Then allow it to go off into other directions. When children relate a story to their own life experiences they better understand its meaning.

The guided reading or listening activity can be used in both small-group and one-to-one story readings, both of which have been found to increase the number and complexity of children's responses as well as their story comprehension (Morrow, 1988). Prompt children to respond, or scaffold and model responses when children do not respond on their own. For example, if a child cannot answer the question, "How did the animals act when the little red hen asked for help?" (Galdone, 1973) say, "Those animals aren't very helpful to the little red hen. Each time she asks them for help they all answer, Not I." Relate the story to your own life experiences, answer questions, and offer positive reinforcement for children's comments. When guided reading takes place in small groups, different formats can be used based on the skill needs of the children. For example, many children are reading in kindergarten and instead of the teacher reading to the children, they can take turns reading. In this case reading materials are carefully matched to the children's reading instructional level.

K-W-L is similar strategy to the guided listening activity but is used a bit more often with informational books because it asks about what learners know about the topic of the book (Ogle, 1986). K-W-L helps to focus reading and listening. K asks, What do I already know about this topic? The W asks, What would I like to find out about the topic? The L is for after listening to the book read or reading the book and asks, What did I learn from the book?

Shared book reading experiences, which take place with the whole class, also encourage children's participation. Pause before predictable phrases, letting children fill them in. "Are you my _____?" from Eastman's (1960) *Are You My Mother?* is a good example. Have children chant stories along with you as you read. Enhance shared book experiences by using Big Books mounted on an easel and designed so that everyone in the class can clearly see words and pictures as the story is read. Use a pointer while reading to reinforce left-to-right progression, the correspondence of spoken and written word, the development of sight vocabulary, and to discuss elements of print that are being studied.

Repeat certain stories to create favorites in your classroom. Children's responses to repeated stories become more sophisticated as they interpret, predict, and make associations with real life. Children begin to narrate familiar stories as the teacher reads; they learn to focus on elements of print, asking names of letters and words.

Follow-up activities help children reconstruct meaning. Retelling engages children in holistic comprehension and organization of thought and allows for personalization. With practice, children learn to introduce a story with its setting and recount its theme, plot episodes, and resolution. Through retelling children demonstrate comprehension of story details and sequence and add inferences and interpretation as well (Morrow, 1997).

Model retelling and encourage use of such reinforcement devices and techniques as verbal prompts, felt boards with story characters, role movies, and puppets (Morrow, 1997b).

Knowledge of Print

RESEARCH.   Mason (1984) suggests that there are three strands of reading behavior that develop separately but concurrently—attention to functions, forms, and conventions of print—with the first of these dominating initial reading development. Children seem to learn how print functions first as they move toward reading (Goodman, 1984; Smith, 1971). Often, the first words a child reads are those with meaning and purpose in the child's life, such as family names, food labels, road signs, and names of fast-food restaurants. Learning about the functions of print has been referred to as the "roots of literacy" (Goodman, 1984). Soon the learner becomes concerned more with the forms of print. This includes detail about names, sounds, and configurations of letters and words. Next children become interested in identifying and using conventions of print. This involves the recognition that print is read from left to right, that punctuation serves certain purposes in printed material, and that spaces serve to separate letters and words. In other words, although recognition of the functions of print seems to dominate reading development at first, the child is at the same time capable of acquiring and learning about the form and conventions of print (Mason, 1984).

Research investigations have made educators very aware of the need to attend to phonemic awareness in early literacy development because research has shown that it is a strong predictor of reading success and is necessary for children to acquire the ability to use phonics (Adams, 1990; Juel, Griffith, & Gough, 1986). Phonemic awareness is the ability to examine language independently of meaning and to manipulate component sounds. It is the awareness that words are composed of smaller units, or phonemes, and requires the ability to attend to a sound in the context of the other sounds in the word. There are levels of difficulty in acquiring this skill; the simplest is the ability to rhyme words and recognize rhyming words. The next level of difficulty involves blending phonemes and splitting syllables (for example segmenting the beginning sound *g* from the rest of the word—*ate*). Finally the most difficult task is segmenting the phonemes in spoken words and manipulating phonemes to form different words (Adams, 1990). Working with strategies like phonics which includes sound-symbol relations, and word-analysis strategies such as context and syntax clues are all considered important in early literacy.

IMPLICATIONS FOR THE KINDERGARTEN PROGRAM.   This research suggests that early instruction in literacy development be focused on the functions of print while concurrently working on the forms of print, including conventions such as phonemic awareness, knowledge of letters, sound-symbol relations, context and syntax clues, syllables, and punctuation.

In kindergarten programs a great deal of emphasis should be placed on the functions of print, such as writing greeting cards or reading print that is related to children's daily lives. Through these experiences children learn the purpose of print and how it is used. They are then able to deal with instruction concerning knowledge of letters and sounds. Although teachers have been concerned about instruction of decoding skills, they are realizing that children do need specific word-recognition strategies to help them become independent readers. A balance between direct instruction in these skills and instruction within the context of real literature, everyday environmental print, and theme units needs to be achieved in order to add meaning to abstract concepts for young children. The development of decoding skills must be put into proper perspective for teachers because it is only one component among a myriad of other experiences necessary in learning how to read.

Writing

RESEARCH.   Writing development begins early and continues along with reading development. Initially children do not differentiate writing from illustration; however, some children as young as 2 years of age differentiate scribble writing from scribble drawing by separating them on the page and explaining which is the picture and which is the story. Their scribble writing progresses to letter-like forms and eventually to discernible letters, often written repeatedly and randomly on a page. At this point some children "invent" spelling before eventually using conventional orthography (Sulzby, 1986). These categories of writing development vary among children, and a given child often will fluctuate back and forth among the categories.

Developing reading skills and writing skills build on each other with each adding to proficiency in the other. Writing was not included in a kindergarten curriculum because it was traditionally perceived as developing after the ability to read. Research in early childhood writing has changed attitudes however, and encouraging writing in preschool and kindergarten and praising children's first attempts to write are now standard practice in early childhood classrooms.

IMPLICATIONS FOR THE KINDERGARTEN PROGRAM.   Children learn to write outside of school and by writing for a purpose, and teachers should keep this in mind in preparing activities for writing. Initiate pen-pal programs with another class or another school, and write invitations to parents, thank-you notes to class visitors, or greeting cards for special occasions. Keep a class address book in the dramatic-play area. Encourage children to collect their Very-own words, words that children decide they want based on home experiences or new school experiences, on 3×5 index cards stored in file boxes or coffee cans. Let children share their thoughts in journals or exchange messages on a bulletin board. The study of themes also generates a reason for writing. Whatever the theme, all of the activities listed previously can be used repeatedly.

In addition, children's literature can be excellent motivation for writing experiences. Series books such as *Madeline* (Bemelmans, 1939) encourage classes or individuals to write their own stories about a central character (Morrow, 1997a).

Many children will not be writing conventionally in kindergarten. We therefore accept and encourage what they can do, including pictures for writing, scribble writing, random letters, invented spelling, and conventional print. It is important to encourage children by letting them know that their unconventional writing is only a beginning, and that it is not the same as the writing that older children can do. Formal instruction in the mechanics of writing letters, spelling, and punctuation can begin with minilessons during the school year.

Literacy-Rich Environments

RESEARCH.   As mentioned already, research from homes where children have come to school already able to read suggests the necessity of a literacy-rich home environment. Taking this information one step further, we need to be very concerned about providing literacy-rich environments in our classrooms. Studies have found that many preschoolers already can read road signs, labels on food boxes, and logos. This finding suggests the importance of providing and using environmental print in classrooms to encourage reading among young children (Goodman, 1984).

IMPLICATIONS FOR THE KINDERGARTEN PROGRAM.   A literacy-rich environment supports and extends literacy development. Classrooms need to be equipped with centers that include materials that encourage reading and writing and help develop themes being studied. Teachers should display and discuss functional print in their classrooms. Classrooms also should include literacy centers with a library corner and a writing area with an abundant supply of materials for reading, writing, and oral-language activities. Dramatic-play centers can be designed to develop literacy as well by including reading and writing materials, for example, when designing a restaurant in which children can role play.

Identify learning centers and each child's cubby with labels. Post daily routines, helper and attendance charts, and a bulletin board for notices of classroom events. Display lists of new words from units of instruction on experience charts, with illustrations next to written words to aid students who are not able to read.

Summary of Research and Implications for Practice

From the research on early literacy it appears there are many areas of development on which to concentrate when designing a program. Skills development should take place in authentic, meaningful settings and in supported and guided-reading settings as well. Research also suggests the concurrent learning of reading, writing, oral language, and listening in a meaningful way through the integration of these skills into play and into content-area teaching such as art, music, math, science, and social studies. This integration can be done through the use of themes that bring meaning and purpose to learning and provide a reason to read, write, listen, and speak. Children's literature should be a major source of these themes. Children also need to have predictable texts with limited vocabularies to begin to read themselves.

These elements need to be organized within the school day to provide whole-group, small-group, and one-to-one instruction. Teachers and students must be involved in ongoing assessment to evaluate progress to plan for instruction. Kindergarten classrooms should be designed to accommodate different organizational structures for learning. Classrooms need literacy and content-area materials for the guided instruction of skills and thematic instruction for integrated learning. The chapters that follow provide a specific framework in which these developmental tools can be used, including examples of organizational structures and activities that can be used to design whole-day and half-day kindergarten programs to maximize early literacy development.

CHAPTER 6

ℳ Framework for the Literacy Curriculum

As we created a framework for the kindergarten literacy curriculum, we found that it had two parts. The first portion focused on literacy skills to be acquired and the experiences important for their acquisition. This portion had a more direct instructional perspective. The second part of the framework looked at the skills and experiences for literacy development within the context of the total curriculum or school day. This portion began with a theme of interest to children and provides activities throughout the content areas to enhance the development of literacy and subject-specific information through inquiry activities such as problem solving and firsthand experiences. We began with the portion of the framework containing the more direct approach and will discuss it in this chapter.

The framework for the literacy curriculum is based on the current research and theoretical perspectives about children's language and literacy development discussed in Chapter 4 and on the observational data we collected in the study that revealed best practices. The first portion of the framework concentrates on the skills and objectives that early childhood teachers feel are important to the acquisition of language and literacy development. In addition to the skills listed in the following pages, children need opportunities for many experiences related to reading and writing. They need these experiences in varied settings with different types of instruction and instructional materials (Strickland, 1990). Objectives for language and literacy learning are necessary for planning instruction and assessing progress. The lists that follow provide the major objectives to include in an early literacy program.

Literacy Objectives for Preparing and Assessing Literacy Instruction

Language Development

ORAL EXPRESSION

1. Speaks in complete sentences.
2. Engages freely in conversation in varied situations.
3. Takes turns appropriately when engaged in conversation.
4. Understands the language of others when spoken to.
5. Pronounces speech sounds and words appropriately for age, language background, and dialect.
6. Has appropriately sized vocabulary for level of maturity.
7. Uses increasingly complex oral language, attending to the structural elements appropriate for age, background, and dialect.
8. Responds to literal and inferential questions.

RECEPTIVE LISTENING

1. Follows oral directions.
2. Attends to adult models of rich oral language.
3. Listens to a variety of literature to increase background information, language of books, and attention span.
4. Attends to others when they are speaking.
5. Discriminates speech sounds appropriately.
6. Discriminates environmental sounds appropriately.
7. Enjoys the rhythm and rhyme of poetry and other literature.
8. Identifies rhyming words.

Reading and Writing Development

POSITIVE ATTITUDES TOWARD READING AND WRITING

1. The child voluntarily chooses to look at books or to write.
2. The child asks to be read to and asks to write.
3. The child listens attentively while being read to and watches others who are writing.
4. The child demonstrates an interest in books by responding to stories read to him or her with questions and comments that are related to the book.

5. The child demonstrates an interest in writing by taking the opportunity to write and sharing what he or she has written with others.

CONCEPTS ABOUT BOOKS

1. Knows that a book is for reading.
2. Knows where the front and back of a book are.
3. Knows which is the top and the bottom of the book.
4. Can turn the pages of a book properly.
5. Knows the difference between the print that is to be read in a book and the pictures.
6. Knows that the pictures on the page are related to what the print says.
7. Can show you where you begin reading on a page.
8. Knows what a title of a book is.
9. Knows what an author is.
10. Knows what an illustrator is.

COMPREHENSION OF TEXT

1. Retells familiar stories using the pictures in the book to help recall the details.
2. Retells stories in reading-like intonations.
3. Can retell a story without the help of the book and demonstrates knowledge of details.
4. Includes elements of story structure in story retelling: setting (beginning, time, place, characters), theme (problem or goal of the main character), plot episodes (events leading toward the main character solving his or her problem or attaining the goal), resolution (problem solved, goal achieved, ending).
5. Responds to story readings with literal, inferential, and critical questions and comments.
6. Story retelling demonstrates inferential and critical insights.
7. Can respond to questions about stories read on literal, interpretive, and critical levels.
8. Participates in story-reading behavior by reciting the story as the teacher reads.
9. Fills in words while being read to based on knowledge of syntax and context.

CONCEPTS ABOUT PRINT

1. Knows that print is read from left to right.
2. Knows that oral language can be written down and then read.
3. Knows what a letter is and can point to one on a printed page.
4. Knows what a word is and can point to one on a printed page.
5. Can read environmental print (signs, familiar store names, and logos).
6. Can recognize some words by sight in the context of book print.
7. Can identify words that rhyme and create rhymes.
8. Can say sounds heard in a word (for example, *cat*: *c* and *at*)
9. Can blend together sounds to form words.
10. Can identify letters by name.
11. Can associate sounds with letters (consonants, vowels, and digraphs).
12. Knows that there are spaces between words.
13. Matches spoken to printed words.
14. Identifies words by sight.
15. Uses syntax, context, and picture clues to identify words.

WRITING

1. Demonstrates the level of development in writing: scribble, drawing for writing, letter-like forms, random letters/letter strings, invented spelling, and conventional spelling.
2. Writes a few words conventionally.
3. Understands the correspondence between spoken and written words in dictation when using dictation to record thoughts.
4. Explores with writing materials.
5. Copies letters and words.
6. Writes his or her name.
7. Collaborates with others in writing.
8. Writes independently.
9. Writes narrative stories and expository information pieces.
10. Uses literature as a model for writing.
11. Writes for functional purposes.
12. Follows the mechanics of writing: forms uppercase letters legibly, forms lowercase letters legibly, writes from left to right, leaves spaces between words, uses capital letters when nec-

essary, uses periods in appropriate places, and uses commas in appropriate places.

Figure 2 provides an illustration of types of reading and writing experiences, settings, instruction, and materials that provide the instructional framework for the more explicit portion of the literacy curriculum. The next section describes each area of the framework in detail.

Types of Reading and Writing Experiences

Children need to experience reading and writing in various ways to learn about these skills from different perspectives. Following are descriptions of types of reading and writing experiences that are important in children's literacy development.

Reading Aloud and Responding

The modeling technique of reading aloud and responding is usually carried out in a whole-group setting. The teacher reads aloud to students and encourages responses to the literature. Students have the opportunity to hear the teacher read with expression and fluency. The selection for reading should be a quality piece of children's literature that is related to themes being addressed in the classroom.

The read-aloud session is structured with before-, during-, and after-reading strategies. The purpose is to enhance comprehension and also to look at elements of print when appropriate.

Before reading, the book is introduced or reintroduced to the children by giving the title and author. Children may be asked to use this information to predict what the story is about. If appropriate, a brief discussion may take place about relevant concepts to be encountered.

During reading, teachers build positive attitudes by showing their own personal pleasure and interest. At times, the teacher may pause and ask the children what they think might happen next or ask them to fill in a predictable word based on the context of the story. Discussion during reading is encouraged as long as it is focused on the story. Children often are invited to read along with the teacher. He or she will encourage them to chant repetitive phrases or narrate the entire text if it is a familiar book that has been read before. In this setting

Figure 2
Strategies & Structures in an Early Literacy Program

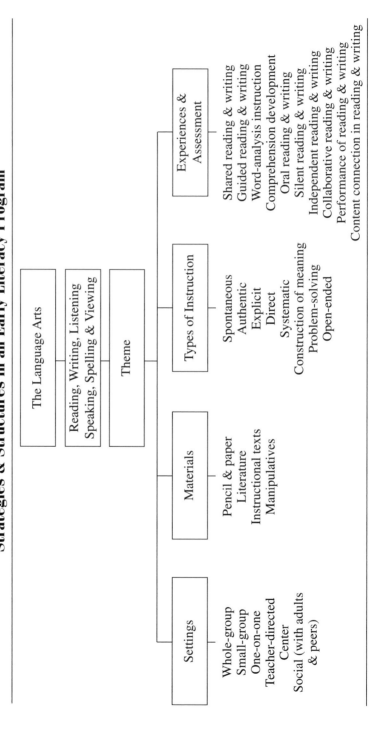

The Language Arts

Reading, Writing, Listening
Speaking, Spelling & Viewing

Theme

Settings

Whole-group
Small-group
One-on-one
Teacher-directed
Center
Social (with adults
& peers)

Materials

Pencil & paper
Literature
Instructional texts
Manipulatives

Types of Instruction

Spontaneous
Authentic
Explicit
Direct
Systematic
Construction of meaning
Problem-solving
Open-ended

**Experiences &
Assessment**

Shared reading & writing
Guided reading & writing
Word-analysis instruction
Comprehension development
Oral reading & writing
Silent reading & writing
Independent reading & writing
Collaborative reading & writing
Performance of reading & writing
Content connection in reading & writing

the teacher often will use a Big Book where the print is visible. The teacher may track the print with his or her hand, a ruler, or a pointer.

After reading, students are encouraged to talk about the story in ways that personalize it for them. They are encouraged to ask questions of the teacher and of one another. Responses to the literature most often come at the end of the reading when children can discuss the story, do a pantomime of a story, role play the story, reenact the story with puppets, or retell the story.

Shared Writing and Reading

Shared writing and reading involves children writing first and then reading what has been written. This happens after the class has participated in an activity related to a topic of discussion or theme being studied. The class usually carries out the shared writing and reading in a whole-group setting, with the teacher as the facilitator and scribe. It begins with a discussion of the activity and then moves to a recording of topics on a chart written by the teacher but dictated by the children. The children are encouraged to use ideas and language relevant to the theme studied, and to join in as the completed chart is read aloud by the teacher.

In addition to dictating the chart, watching the teacher write it, and reading it, in shared writing and reading the children look at elements of the text with the teacher. The class is asked to look for letters and words they recognize, words and letters that are repeated, punctuation marks, and other features of interest to them. If the class is learning about rhymes, words can be selected from the chart for children to supply a rhyming word. If the class has been working on specific consonant letter-sound relations, they can be asked to find them in the chart. The shared writing and reading should end by going back to the whole-group setting and rereading the entire chart together (Strickland, 1989).

Guided Reading and Writing

Guided reading and writing usually will take place in a small-group setting or on a one-to-one basis with teacher and child. Children are grouped based on their similar needs in literacy instruction. The teacher acts as a mentor and a coach, offering explicit instruction and styling learning to meet the individual needs of children. The materials selected and activities carried out are designed specifically to meet an individual child's needs and instructional level for learning.

There are particular outlines for guided reading lessons; however, they can vary depending on the age of the children involved and their needs. Guided reading can include the development of fluent reading, comprehension skills, word-recognition skills, and writing skills. The traditional guided reading lesson includes children reading or being read something that is easy and familiar for fluency and success. The child often selects the book to read or listen to among many with which he or she is already familiar. With kindergarten children, it may be a story children have heard, and they will read the story from the pictures rather than the print, in attempted reading behavior.

While the child is reading or pretend reading the teacher keeps a running record to evaluate progress in word analysis. This record allows the teacher to follow the text as the child is reading. He or she marks errors and evaluates the type of miscue the child is making to help him or her with strategies to improve independent fluent reading. Familiar materials provide a good opportunity to discuss the story being read with the aim of enhancing comprehension development.

Children practice writing words they know or are working on, writing on small chalkboards or white boards. When children do not write conventional words yet, they can use scribble writing, letter strings, or invented spelling. Additional work with words occurs as children learn about parts of words, including common word endings, using magnetic letters, or a small slate or white board. In kindergarten they will work on rhyming words, determining how many sounds they hear in a word, sounding parts of words, and blending them together to enhance phonemic awareness.

In guided reading lessons children also write their own stories in a notebook or log. Again, depending on the children's level of literacy development, they may scribble write or use letter strings or invented spelling. Elements of print are attended to in the child's writing, including letters in their name or other letters they may know.

Finally, a new book that is selected by the teacher is introduced. The teacher discusses what the story is about and looks at the pictures with the child to predict what the people or animals might say in the story. Words from the story are also discussed. The teacher may read the story first, but sometimes the child will do it alone if he or she is capable. The teacher helps the child with strategies for decoding if he or she is having difficulty figuring out words. In kindergarten children may be reading the book from the pictures or from remembering what the teacher read to them. A discussion about the book follows.

There are many variations to the steps in a guided reading lesson; however, what is most important is to learn as much as possible about the children you are working with to provide them with appropriate materials and provide them with new strategies in this small-group setting.

Independent Reading and Writing Alone or in Collaboration

In an early literacy program children should have time to engage in literacy learning without the teacher, both alone and in a socially interactive way with other children. Working independent of the teacher promotes self-direction, sense of responsibility, and self-empowerment. This opportunity also provides children with practice in reading and writing for fluency and for pleasure.

When deciding to work alone or in collaboration with others, children can select among several literacy choices. This piece of the school day can be called literacy-center time. Introduce the literacy center and literacy-center time by explaining the use of a small number of activities available to the children. Eventually add items to the area as children become used to working without the assistance of the teacher. The first day that the children use the literacy center, for example, you can introduce the open-faced book shelves, the system for book selection, and materials for making their own books. On another day introduce the literature manipulative materials such as the felt board and story characters and taped stories with headsets. On subsequent days additional activities can be added. Introducing a few materials at a time avoids confusion. The following strategies are designed to facilitate literacy-center time.

1. Stress that the classroom be relatively quiet, with minimal movement during literacy-center time.

2. Introduce new books and other materials as they are added to the center areas.

3. Explain how to care for books and other materials, showing where they are located in the classroom library corner so that everyone knows where to find them and where to return them.

4. Provide a list of literacy-center activities on a checksheet where children can indicate their choices of things to do for a given literacy-center period. Use rebus pictures to indicate activities, and help children identify them if they cannot read the chart. When children have selected their activities to do during the literacy-center period in advance, they know where to go and what to do.

5. Encourage children to stay with their choices for the entire literacy-center session, allowing them to change once or twice if they wish.

6. Allow children to work alone or with other children in the literacy center, at their desk or table, or at other locations in the classroom.

7. Restate often the objectives of the literacy-center time: to read and enjoy reading and to write and enjoy writing.

Materials for writing, binding, and illustrating books can be put to use by students during this time, as can student journals, logs, individual record keeping, and checking books in or out to take home. Children can lead discussions about books, authors, or illustrations with other children. They can engage in storyreading or storytelling with the literature manipulatives. The literacy center provides manipulative hands-on materials related to literature, with many choices so that children who are not ready to sit down and read can immerse themselves in literature in a way that they can enjoy.

In one of our observations during literacy-center time children, some with stuffed animals clutched under their arms, were reading alone but side by side as they relaxed on soft pillows. One child read to another snuggled in the box called the "private spot." Two children used a felt board to tell a story—one manipulated the felt characters as the other read.

A group listened on headsets to a taped story of *The Little Red Hen*, following the words in the books as they listened. Because the tape was audible only to the children with the headsets, it was amusing to suddenly hear them chanting along at the part in the story when the animals say, "Not I." Two other children were writing letters to their pen pals, a few were checking out books to take home, and others were comparing the number of books they had read. One child was pretending to be the teacher and read a story to a group. Another child asked if he could have a turn at being the teacher.

At the beginning of the period the teacher made sure that the children were involved. She read to a small group who asked to hear a story. She observed a few youngsters acting out *The Three Billy Goats Gruff* with finger puppets. After that she sat down with her own novel and read, modeling her own interest in books.

Performance of Reading and Writing Accomplishments

When students accomplish reading and writing activities, whether independent or collaborative efforts, they should have the opportunity to share what they have done. This can be done in a most informal manner, with a partner or small group, for the teacher or the entire class. Being able to share reading and writing that has been completed provides intrinsic rewards for students and gives more meaning and purpose to the task.

Assessing Performance

During guided reading with individual children or in small groups the teacher takes notes and records anecdotes of children's behavior. These notes become part of the records on each child's progress and help in the prescription of future work. Teachers create folders for maintaining the records for each of the students in his or her classroom. Other materials to place in the folders include periodic samples of children's drawings, writing, and tapes or transcribed samples of oral language. Assessment measures used in the study, such as story retellings and tests of concepts about books and print can be a part of the assessment folder as well. Lists of objectives for oral language, writing, and reading development presented earlier in this chapter can be duplicated in checklist form for each child. The teacher can use this as a guide for observing development. The list of skills at the beginning of this chapter can be used as a checklist for assessment. In

Chapter 5 there is a description of measures used to evaluate student achievement. The measures included in Appendix B such as The Kindergarten Inventory, The Story Retelling Test, and Story Reenactment Test all can be used as assessment tools by the teacher to add to the material in each child's folder.

Organizing Instructional Settings to Meet Individual Needs

Once the elements of a program have been identified, organizing the instruction becomes a crucial concern. The best plans could end up being unsuccessful due to poor management. There are a variety of strategies for organizing instruction. Children can be taught in whole-class lessons, in small groups, and individually. Many different grouping techniques can be used. Children can be grouped for ability (homogeneous grouping) or they can be grouped heterogeneously in interest groups, skill groups, or, using cooperative learning, in peer groups. The use of a variety of organizational strategies is important because some children benefit from one setting more than another. Grouping children in a variety of arrangements eliminates the stigmas attached to a single grouping system and allows children to interact with all children in the class. Grouping is based on instructional needs; long-term ability grouping is avoided (Strickland, 1995). Using varied organizational strategies provides a more interesting educational experience.

Grouping Practices

Whole-group lessons are appropriate when a subject being taught needs to be learned by all children and will be understood by all children in a large-group presentation. Reading stories, singing songs, and class discussions are appropriate whole-group activities that promote literacy development.

Small-group instruction is effective when teaching specific skills that require careful supervision or close interaction with children. Appropriate literacy lessons for small groups might be a directed listening and thinking activity with a comprehension objective that involves interpretive and critical thinking. The cooperative project could be creating pictures for group book based on a particular topic, or assignment to a particular center because all children cannot fit in one area at one time. Teachers often select groups of children who have similar needs for skill development because it allows the opportunity to work closely with a few children who are both at the same literacy level and who have the same needs. Grouping based on development of skills in an area where children demonstrate similar needs is more appropriate than homogeneous grouping based on a general test of ability. Organizing groups with children who have similar needs will make grouping meaningful because it is based on a specific purpose. Groups must also be flexible because they are formed to accomplish a goal and disband, with new groups forming when necessary. This flexible arrangement for grouping allows children to work with many other children and eliminates stigmas often attached to fixed homogeneous grouping that assigns ability labels to groups. When children as young as 4 years old are organized into high, middle, and low instructional groups that stay the same for an entire school year, they are as aware of their group placement as children in third or fourth grade.

In addition to the teacher-organized groups, children should be given the opportunity to select groups in which they might like to be based on interest and friendships.

Individual Instruction

Working one on one and allowing children to work independently are two forms of individualized instruction. Although children need to work with peers in cooperative ways and they learn a great deal from a social interactive environment, working with youngsters on a one-to-one basis offers the child personal attention and the opportunity for the teacher to learn a great deal about him or her. The appropriate types of literacy activities in which to involve a child for one-to-one instruction are story retelling, attempted readings of a favorite storybook, helping with specific skill needs such as learning letters of the alphabet or color identification, assessing knowledge a child has acquired, reading stories to children with prompts for them to question and comment about the story, and taking dictation of original stories or helping children themselves to write. Many activities that are appropriate for individualized instruction also can be used in small-group settings.

Teachers may wish to meet with children on a one-on-one basis regularly. This type of meeting, if done regularly, can prove to be extremely productive for the teacher and child. A 20-minute period called *conference time* can be set aside daily for individual meetings between teacher and child. The teacher can meet with every child about once a week for at least a few minutes. At conference time teachers can assess children's needs, record accomplishments, give instruction, and assign tasks until the next meeting. Children who are already reading will have reading lessons during the conference period, and other children might be given instruction dealing with the ability to differentiate between the print and the pictures in a book. In another conference, the teacher may read a story to the child and encourage responses and questions during the reading. The teacher will choose to do the one-to-one storybook readings with children who have not had the opportunity to be read to at home. The content of the conference is determined by the needs and interests of the child. Children from age 3 and older can participate in conferences, and their maturity determines exactly how the conference is carried out. A typical conference will last 5 minutes, but it can be as short as 2 minutes and as long as 15 minutes. The conference should have an informal atmosphere and is usually a special time for both teacher and child, giving them the opportunity to build a rapport.

The necessity for meeting with children in very small groups of no more than three or on a one-to-one basis becomes apparent to teachers. In one kindergarten classroom, a mother expressed the fact that her child liked to be absent from school. She went on to say that he liked to be absent because when he returned to school he was given "private time" with the teacher. Evidently there was something special for this child to meet with the teacher alone. When working with children on a one-on-one basis for only a few minutes a week, teachers learn what children know, what they want to know, and what they need to know.

Self-Directed Learning

In addition to assessing children's needs and providing instruction during conferences, the teacher assigns work for children to be done by the next time he or she sees the child. The work is designed for each child's interests and needs and usually involves the use of some material at a center in the room. The work assignment serves two purposes: it allows children practice in areas with which they need help, and it begins to instill responsibility for accomplishing assigned tasks.

To make the assignment official and to help children remember what it is they are to do, a contract or assignment sheet is made up for them. Because most of the children we are discussing are not able to read, the contract is composed of pictures and words. The teacher and child check off the areas in which the child is to work, and at the next conference they read over the contract and check what the child has done. Typical assignments might be to read a book in the library corner, to read over one's own words, to copy words from a new word list, and to make a book of pictures about the topic being studied.

During self-directed learning times, students can use the literacy center as discussed earlier, work with own words, listen to books on headsets, or work at creating a book. They should have practice working independently if the teacher is to hold individual conferences. Montessori schools are effective in making young children independent, self-directed, and able to work individually or in small groups without the need for the teacher's direct involvement. They use manipulative learning materials that are placed in centers on accessible shelves. Teachers illustrate the use of materials before placing them on the shelves unless they are self-explanatory, and each material has its own place. Before selecting a new material to work with, the child must replace the one that he or she is using. Only certain materials are allowed for use during conference periods: those that are relatively quiet, that can be used independently, and that may have been assigned for use for a particular child. During the first few weeks of school, teachers introduce conference-time materials and allow children to work with them. When the children are capable of functioning independently, the teacher will begin to hold conferences while the rest of the children work independently. The teacher will announce who will be seen during the conference period before it begins and write the names of the children on the board. At the end of the conference period, the children who will be seen the next day are mentioned and their names are written on the chalkboard.

A Final Thought

It is important that the teacher use a variety of organizational strategies to meet individual learning styles and to make the school day more interesting through a variety of instructional settings. In teaching children in groups and on a one-to-one basis, the teacher may not seem to be creating a literacy environment for reading to occur naturally because these arrangements are somewhat structured. We have learned, however, that relying completely on a child's initiative and expecting that learning will occur is not realistic. We need to plan for children and support their learning.

We have outlined the necessary skills to teach kindergarten students and an instructional framework. We now need to think about how to integrate these elements throughout the school day. The next chapter addresses this integration.

CHAPTER 7

A Framework for Integrating Literacy Into Content-Area Teaching

Having examined early literacy perspectives, skills to be learned in the literacy program, and guided instruction in these skill areas, it is important to focus on the integration of literacy activities throughout the school day. This chapter provides the second part of the framework for the literacy curriculum and focuses on why and how it is important to integrate literacy activities throughout the school day.

Integrating Literacy Activities Throughout the Curriculum

The concept of the integrated school day, an interdisciplinary approach to teaching of content, is very much associated with educational reformer John Dewey. He suggested that learning should be based on the interests of the child, and that it should be active, manipulative, and sensory oriented. He believed that children need time to explore, experiment, and play in a classroom filled with interesting materials in order to learn. Dewey suggested that education should be based on real-life experiences and that through the pursuit of their interests and activities children would participate in skill development that could occur in a functional way (Dewey, 1966). For example, if the class is studying dinosaurs, dinosaurs are discussed, read about, written about, created out of clay in art, sung about at music time, and counted in math. Children in this situation become interested in a topic and use that interest as a motivator to learn other skills.

The integration of content-area study to teach early literacy skills therefore includes concern for children's interests and individual differences. It provides socially interactive settings and behaviors to model and emulate. It centers around life experiences, has a purpose, and is functional. Along with the more direct instructional model described in the previous chapter, our kindergarten model includes the interdisciplinary approach for the acquisition of skills.

The concept of theme-based instruction has moved away from merely guiding students through a series of activities that focus on a specific topic. Today's teachers focus more on developing children's sense of inquiry; that is, their ability to develop questions about a topic, determine ways to find answers to their questions, and share what they learn with others. Kindergarten children can be exposed to areas of interest through firsthand experiences and through read-aloud sessions. Their curiosity is aroused as they learn about new topics and generate new questions for further learning, and use various resources (for example, more read aloud, simple experimentation, and questioning others) to build their information base and share what they know with the group. Rather than simply isolating the activities into subject areas, content areas more naturally come into play as children learn about the world around them. They use math to answer certain questions. They write, dictate, or draw pictures that relate to questions for others to answer or to record their own answers. They discuss what they know and what they want to find out. The processes of listening, speaking, reading, writing, and thinking are used in an integrated way as they learn more about the topic.

In developing our framework, we began with a map for which the teachers could select a theme (see Figure 3). We then thought about all content areas and their related skills to be learned. Activities were designed to meet the needs of content-area objectives and literacy objectives and then scheduled throughout the day. The maps provided were tools to help the teachers use the framework.

In the following sections we discuss objectives for different curriculum areas and what they mean for practice. In each area we indicate how literacy experiences are incorporated as well, and how children have the opportunity to engage with new language to enhance

Figure 3
Daily Schedule Planning Sheet

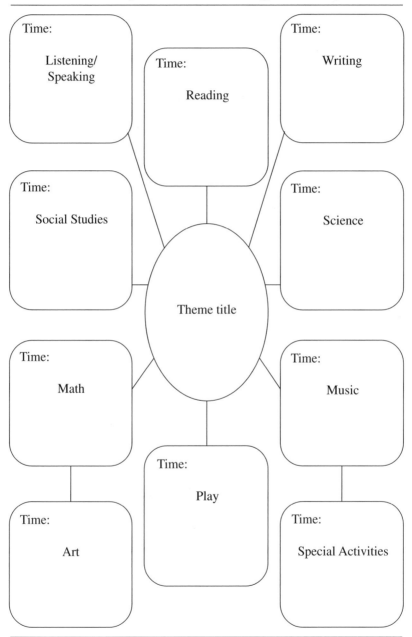

vocabulary and syntax. There are many experiences with storybooks related to the theme that promote comprehension and enjoyment. Writing about the theme with some meaningful purpose is also an integral part of the experience.

Art and Literacy

In kindergarten, art experiences should offer children a variety of opportunities including exposure to varied art materials, exploration and experimentation with these materials, expression of feeling through art, representation of experiences through visual forms, appreciation for varied art forms, naming and discussing content of art (line, color, texture, form, and shape), and the experience of literacy learning in art activities.

Art experiences provide a time for rich oral language to be used. If children are encouraged to converse while involved in these experiences, language will flourish. When one listens to preschoolers and kindergartners immersed in finger painting, words such as *mushy*, *slushy*, *gushy*, and *squiggles* are likely to be heard. When children play with play dough and clay, words such as *pound*, *squeeze*, *roll*, *press*, and *fold* will enter the conversation. A child is often anxious to show what he or she has created and asks another student to look at the creation. This is likely to result in children asking one another how they made their projects. Describing the process to each other provides excellent practice for language development. Water color paints stimulate comments such as "Oooh, it's drippy," "The paint is running down the page like a stream of water," "Look how the colors all run together, the red is making the blue turn purple," and "My picture looks like a rainbow of colors across the sky."

The teacher can take the opportunity to make word lists from the language that is generated in art activities, to encourage the children to share and talk about what they are doing. The words that individual children generate are a source for their Very-own word collections. Children sometimes like to dictate a sentence or story about their artwork, or begin to write about it themselves. Individual works of art about a similar topic can be bound together in a book for children to look at and read, if print has been used with the pictures. It is appropriate to highlight concepts being taught, such as emphasizing the letter *P* in art activities, thus connecting the abstract concept of a letter to something that has meaning for a child. For example, when teaching the letter *P*, use purple paint, purple paper, purple play dough, and purple felt-tipped markers.

Music and Literacy

Kindergarten music experiences can provide a means for literacy development and should include intense involvement in and response to music; exposure to different forms of music (instruments, singing, types of music) to help children learn to discriminate among them and develop an appreciation for varied forms; music experiences that involve listening, singing, moving, playing, and creating; expressing feelings through music experiences; and experiencing literacy learning in music activities.

During music experiences, children use new language found in songs and increase their vocabulary. Songs emphasize syllabic patterns in words that should be brought to the attention of children. Take the opportunity to write songs on experience chart paper and sing them while you point to the words for the children to see. Picture story books that illustrate songs such as "Old MacDonald Had a Farm" provide predictable reading material for young children. Listening to classical music often creates images and is a rich source for language. Children can invent stories around the music. They can describe the music with emotional words or sentences. Describing the sounds of instruments played on a tape also creates some interesting language.

Play and Literacy

In kindergarten, play experiences include providing opportunities for children to problem solve, acquire new understandings, role play real-life experiences, cope with situations that require sharing and cooperating, and develop language and literacy through play.

Dramatic play provides endless possibilities for literacy development in oral language, written language, and reading. The materials that are usually found in the dramatic-play area will generate considerable language, but the teacher can take the opportunity to add items to ensure as much use of print as possible. One of the reasons that it is crucial to use this area for reading, writing, and oral language is that it provides real-life settings and functional reasons for using print.

Studying different units dealing with social studies and science is a time for added print-related materials. The study of community helpers is a familiar topic for early childhood teachers. Some of the popular helpers we discuss are firemen, policemen, supermarket workers, doctors, nurses, postal workers, and office workers. The selection of any of these community helpers provides the opportunity to add literacy materials to the dramatic-play area. For example, to foster use of print when learning about how people function in operating the supermarket the teacher can add the following items to the dramatic-play area: a selection of empty food cans, food boxes, and detergent containers; a toy cash register, play money, and note pads for taking orders; a telephone; store signs that post hours; advertisements for special purchases; and food posters. A good idea is for the teacher to visit the supermarket to note the environmental print and try to duplicate some of it in the classroom. It may be possible to pick up some of the signs and posters (store managers will give them away when they no longer have use for them). Include a supermarket bookshelf with magazines and books for sale. Children will use these materials to engage in conversation as they role play as store manager, clerk, and shopper. They will write down orders and read posters, signs, and books that have been placed there. They may make their own shopping lists or make new signs when they are required. A great deal of active involvement in all areas of literacy can occur in a center such as this. At least once a month throughout the school year, change the dramatic-play area into another setting using all the print materials usually found in that environment.

Social Studies, Science, and Literacy

In kindergarten, social studies experiences should include fostering self-esteem; learning social skills for functioning, such as sharing, cooperating, and communicating with others; recognizing and respecting similarities and differences in others; increasing knowledge of other cultures and ethnic groups; increasing understanding of the nature of our social world through the study of history, geography, and economics;

and using the content of social studies to promote literacy development. Science experiences should include observing, hypothesizing, recording data, surmising, analyzing, and drawing conclusions; increasing understanding in biological science (the study of living things) and physical science (including the study of astronomy and weather); and using the content of science to promote literacy development.

Science and social studies are two content areas that provide the greatest opportunity for literacy development. The content generates enthusiasm, meaning, and a purpose for using emergent literacy strategies. For example, studying a farm involves both social studies and science, and oral language can be developed through discussions about work on the farm, different types of farms, and animals on the farm. Word lists can be made of farm animals, farm crops, or jobs on the farm. Pictures depicting farm scenes also will generate discussion as will a trip to a farm or a visit from a farmer who talks about his or her work.

To encourage positive attitudes toward books, the teacher can carefully select good pieces of children's literature to read to the class about farms. *Petunia* (Duvoisin, 1950) is a delightful story about a goose who lives on a farm. *The Little Red Hen* (Galdone, 1973), *Peter Rabbit* (Potter, 1902), *Little Farm* (Lenski, 1965), and *Charlie Needs a Clock* (dePaola, 1973) are just a few samples of good children's literature that relate to the farm and will interest children in wanting to look at the books after they have been read to them. Story readings can help develop children's learning about print. Children can be asked to retell the stories, role play the stories, and participate in the story reading with some type of shared book experience that allows them to participate in the reading of the book. Discussion before and after the story reading and discussions held in small-group readings provide a child with the opportunity to construct meaning around the text.

As a result of a visit to the farm, children can draw pictures and dictate sentences about their farm illustration. The pictures can be bound into a class book and read by the entire class. Teachers can generate language experience lessons as a result of the farm unit by having children dictate experience charts about what they have learned. Very-own farm words should be elicited from the children to add to their collection of words. The teacher should take the opportunity to make associations of letters and sounds that are in words generated by the children that relate to the farm with letters and sounds that are found in children's names and that are being discussed. When literacy learning is abstract, as in the instance of letters and sounds, it is important to associate it with meaningful, interesting, and functional experiences.

Science experiments and food preparation related to topics being studied offer opportunities for more discussion, such as the generation of interesting words for word lists and writing recipe charts, experiment directions, and results of experiments based on observations and outcomes experienced.

The block-play center is also an area that will stimulate the need for print materials and language by adding interesting new items when they are being studied. If transportation is the topic being discussed, toy trucks, trains, cars, boats, and airplanes should be added to the block corner. Other additions could include tickets for traveling on these modes of transportation, tags for marking luggage, or maps for making travel plans. Travel brochures and posters and environmental signs that are commonly found at airports and train stations including gate numbers, names of airlines, and arrival and departure signs also would be appropriate. These kinds of materials will encourage building airports and train stations with blocks and the use of the print-related materials to enhance the block play.

Mathematics and Literacy

Mathematics experiences in kindergarten should include activities that involve many opportunities to handle and deal with mathematical materials and ideas; movement from dependence on the concrete to abstract ideas; opportunities to classify, compare, seriate, measure, graph, count, identify, and write numbers and perform operations on numbers; using mathematical vocabulary; and using mathematics to promote literacy development.

In all of the other content areas, a teacher can feel confident that he or she is providing an adequate program of study through the themed units that incorporate music, art, play, and literacy development. However, math, like literacy, is a specialized area that needs more attention than can be given in a content-area unit. Yet there are many activities that bring meaning to mathematics through unit topics that include literacy. The teacher can read stories related to numbers, children can count out cookies for snack to make sure there are enough for the class, and children can be in charge of collecting and counting milk money. When studying weather, the class can create a chart of daily temperatures to observe the variability from day to day.

Benefits of Integrated Units

When literacy skills are developed in an integrated fashion, as in the practices and approaches described in this chapter, children see purposes and reasons for becoming literate. Teachers also must have time for direct instruction of reading in guided reading lessons in order to meet the individual needs of all children.

When we teach literacy skills void of content and real-life experience, the child perceives the activity as not being useful. When taught in an integrated or interdisciplinary fashion, the children ask for the skills that they consider necessary to participate fully in experiences that are of interest to them during their work and play at school.

When observing a kindergarten class during a unit on transportation where some of the materials described were made available to the children, we noted that many children asked for more materials as a result of their participation in the block-play center. Children looked at books that were available about transportation and requested to have some on space travel that had not been included before. Other children wanted maps of places not included in the center. Many children requested particular Very-own words. Children asked for help preparing signs that they needed to represent places to which they wanted to travel and highway signs indicating mileage to the next stop. Some children also were involved in dictating directions to get from one place to the next. The need for literacy information was created by the teacher's preparation of the environment, which included interesting and real-life experiences. In this environment learning becomes self-generated.

Guidelines for Planning and Implementing Units

Unit themes can be selected by the teacher and the children. Giving students choices concerning what they will learn is important. When a topic is selected, allow the children to brainstorm what they

Figure 4
Curriculum Web for a Thematic Unit on Nutrition

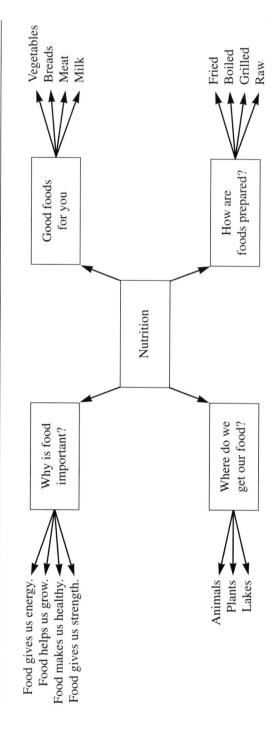

From Lesley M. Morrow, *Literacy Development in the Early Years: Helping Children Read and Write* (3rd Edition). Copyright 1997 by Allyn & Bacon. Reprinted by permission.

would like to know about. You might begin by suggesting categories on which to focus and letting the class fill in subheadings (Rand, 1994). In preparation for a unit on nutrition, we asked a class of kindergarten children to help decide what they might like to learn. We used a web to chart their ideas and started it for them with nutrition as the theme and four categories on which to focus: Why is food important? What foods are good for you? Were do we get food from? and How are different foods prepared to eat? The web in Figure 4 illustrates the children's responses and the content to be studied for the unit.

In planning the unit, the teacher should include activities in all content areas. The map in Figure 4 will help to generate activities related to the unit topic and include each of the content areas. From this map the teacher can select activities to schedule throughout the school day.

We have included a complete integrated language arts unit in Appendix A that illustrates how teachers can use content areas to teach literacy skills and information about themes.

With the objectives, structures, and themes in place, the total picture for literacy development in the kindergarten is almost complete. The next aspect to consider is the physical environment of the classroom and how it can support the instruction we have described.

CHAPTER 8

Creating a Framework for Literacy-Rich Environments

Mrs. Bailey's kindergarten class was learning about workers in the community. The children decided during a discussion of news reporters that they would like to have a news office in the dramatic-play area where they could publish their own paper. Their teacher helped create the center where they placed writing paper, telephones, phone directories, a typewriter, and a computer. The corner's materials also included pamphlets, maps, and other appropriate reading material for the different sections of the newspaper, such as sports, travel, weather, and general daily news. When the class had completed their first newspaper, Jonathan was the class member in charge of delivering it. He had a newspaper delivery bag filled with papers, each with the name of a child on it. Jonathan had to match the names on the papers to the names on the children's cubbies. Later when the kindergartners read their newspapers, they shared them with great enthusiasm. Each child had contributed something to the paper, whether it was a drawing, a story, or a group poem.

This example illustrates children participating in functional literacy activities. The classroom environment was prepared with materials and space that stimulated reading and writing.

Although the learning environment often is viewed as background or scenery for teaching and learning, there is another way to discuss the physical setting and the teacher's role in creating it. This view recognizes that in arranging the environment purposefully, teachers acknowledge the physical setting as an important influence on their activities, as well as those of the children. Appropriate physical arrangement of furniture, selection of materials, and the aesthetic quality of a room provide a space that contributes to learning and teaching.

In this chapter, we describe a physical environment that supports optimum literacy development in kindergarten classrooms. The discussion of spaces and materials will concentrate mostly on the development of reading, writing, and oral language. The overall concept is to promote literacy as an interdisciplinary pursuit integrated throughout the school day.

Perspectives Concerning Literacy-Rich Environments

Motivation theory suggests that access to and choice of materials that are challenging and offer opportunities for success will encourage students to engage in activities (in this case literacy activities) in a voluntary and sustained manner. Therefore the physical environment in a classroom can play a large role in motivating children to read and write. When designing classrooms teachers should consider many elements of motivation theory including the meaning and function of the materials for the students. Teachers also should think about conceptual orientation; that is, materials should be connected to content-area subjects or a theme to add interest. There should be many *choices* of materials and activities that provide a challenge but lead to success, and the materials must be accessible so that students can use them easily. The environment needs to be designed for social interaction among peers and adults.

As mentioned in Chapter 7, historically, philosophers who studied early childhood development described the importance of preparing the environment with manipulative materials to foster learning in real-life settings (Froebel, 1974; Rusk & Scotland, 1979). Montessori (1965) advocated carefully prepared classrooms with every material in the environment attached to a specific learning objective to promote independent learning.

Research studies also have demonstrated how the physical design of classrooms affects children's behavior. Rooms partitioned into small spaces facilitate verbal interaction and cooperative play among peers more than rooms with large open spaces (Field, 1980). Children in carefully arranged rooms have shown more creative productivity and greater use of language-related activities than children in randomly arranged rooms (Moore, 1986). Literacy-enriched dramatic-play areas based on themes have stimulated literacy activities and enhanced literacy skills (Morrow & Rand, 1991; Neuman & Roskos, 1992). Dramatic play with story props has improved comprehension of stories including recall of details and the ability to sequence and interpret (Mandler & Johnson, 1977). Enhancing physical designs of literacy centers has increased children's use of materials in the centers and the children's literacy achievement as well (Morrow, 1992).

Arranging the Classroom to Motivate Reading and Writing

Although there is no single way to effectively arrange a classroom, the following plan is suggested as a guide. As mentioned in Chapter 7, a rich literacy environment should include a literacy center with a library corner and writing area abundant with materials to encourage literacy development. Literacy-rich classrooms also contain centers dedicated to content areas, such as social studies, science, math, art, music, dramatic play, block play, and literacy. The checklist in Figure 5 will help teachers determine if they have included all necessary elements.

Centers contain general materials pertinent to each content area and materials specific to topics being studied. Literacy materials are included in all centers that are designed so children can use them independently or in small groups. Centers are accessible as are the materials in them that are stored on shelves or in boxes. The materials are labeled, and each piece has a designated spot so that teachers can direct children to specific items and so that children can find and return them easily. Early in a school year, centers hold a small number of items, with new materials added as the year progresses. When new items are placed in centers, teachers introduce their purpose, use, and placement (Montessori, 1965)

The room design supports whole-group, small-group, and individual instruction. A conference table provides space for small-group

Figure 5
Checklist for Evaluating the Literacy Environment

The Literacy Center
- ☐ Children participate in designing the center (develop rules, select a name for center, and develop materials.)
- ☐ Area placed in a quiet section of the room.
- ☐ Visually and physically accessible, yet partitioned from the rest of the room.
- ☐ Rug, throw pillows, rocking chair, bean bag chair, and stuffed animals.
- ☐ Private spot in the corner such as a box to crawl into and read.
- ☐ The center uses about 10% of the classroom space and fits five to six children.

The Library Corner
- ☐ Bookshelves for storing books with spines facing outward.
- ☐ Organizational system for shelving books.
- ☐ Open-faced bookshelves for featured books.
- ☐ Five to eight books per child.
- ☐ Books represent three to four grade levels of the following types: (a) picture books, (b) picture storybooks, (c) traditional literature, (d) poetry, (e) realistic literature, (f) informational books, (g) biographies, (h) chapter books, (i) easy to read books, (j) riddle and joke books, (k) participation books, (l) series books, (m) textless books, (n) television-related books, (o) brochures, (p) magazines, and (q) newspapers.
- ☐ Twenty new books circulated every 2 weeks.
- ☐ Check-out/check-in system for children to take out books daily.
- ☐ Head sets and taped stories.
- ☐ Felt board and story characters with related books.
- ☐ Materials for constructing felt stories.
- ☐ Other story manipulatives (roll movie or puppets with related books).
- ☐ System for recording books read (for example, 3 × 5 cards hooked onto a bulletin board).

The Writing Center (The Author's Spot)
- ☐ Tables and chairs.
- ☐ Writing posters and a bulletin board for children to display their writing themselves.
- ☐ Writing utensils (pens, pencils, crayons, felt-tipped markers, and colored pencils).
- ☐ Writing materials (many varieties of paper in all sizes, booklets, and pads).
- ☐ Typewriter or computer.

(continued)

Figure 5
Checklist for Evaluating the Literacy Environment
(continued)

☐ Materials for writing stories and making them into books.
☐ A message board for children to post messages for the teacher and students.
☐ A place to store Very-own words.
☐ Folders for children to place samples of their writing.

Content-Area Learning Centers
☐ Environmental print, such as signs related to themes, directions, and rules.
☐ A calendar.
☐ A current-events board.
☐ Appropriate books, magazines, and newspapers in all centers.
☐ Writing utensils in all centers.
☐ Varied types of paper in all centers.
☐ A place for children to display their literacy work.

and individualized instruction for skill development. The conference table is placed in a quiet area of the room and is situated so the teacher also can see the children who are working independently at centers.

Centers are positioned so areas where quiet work is typical (literacy, math, social studies, and science) are away from more noisy, active environments (dramatic-play and blocks centers) (see Figure 6).

Visually Accessible Environmental Print

Content-area classrooms are filled with functional print such as labels on materials. Signs communicate information, for example, *Quiet Please* and *Please Put Materials Away After Using Them.* Charts labeled Helpers, Daily Routines, Attendance, and Calendar simplify classroom management (Morrow, 1997a; Schickedanz, 1993). A notice board is used to communicate in writing with the children. Experience charts display new words generated from themes, recipes, and science experiments. Environmental print must be *used* or it will go unnoticed. Children are encouraged to read it, copy it, and use the word labels in their writing.

The Literacy Center

The literacy center is composed of a library corner and author's spot (see Figure 7). The center should be visually attractive with children having easy access to books. Children read and write more in classrooms with literacy centers than children whose classrooms do

Figure 6
Early Childhood Classroom Floor Plan

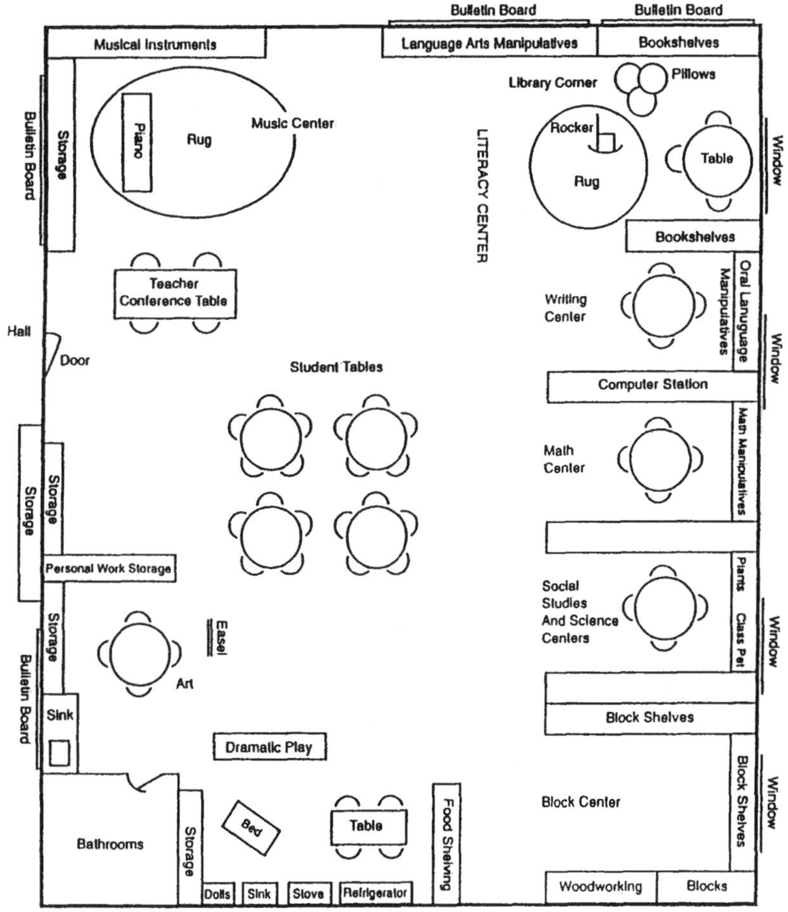

From Lesley M. Morrow, *Literacy Development in the Early Years: Helping Children Read and Write* (3rd Edition). Copyright 1997 by Allyn & Bacon. Reprinted by permission.

Figure 7
The Literacy Center

From L.M. Morrow, 1997. *The Literacy Center: Contexts for Reading and Writing.* York, Maine: Stenhouse Publishers. Used with permission.

not have them (Morrow, 1992). Involve children in designing and managing the literacy center, letting them help develop rules for its use and keeping it neat and orderly (Morrow, 1997b).

LIBRARY CORNER.   A classroom library corner gives children immediate access to books (Morrow & Weinstein, 1986). The library corner should be inviting but should afford privacy and be clearly defined as a discrete area. House most books on shelves with only their spines showing, but include an open-faced bookshelf to feature special books. Use a coding system to help children learn that books in regular libraries are organized systematically for easy access.

Include five to eight books per child at three or four different grade levels and include picture storybooks, fables, fairy tales, informational books, magazines, poetry, and novels. Stock multiple copies of popular books and replace about 25 books every 2 weeks, either with new books or with books used earlier. Devise an easy check-out system so that books can be taken home from the classroom library.

Make the library corner comfortable with pillows, a rocking chair, a rug, a table, and chairs at which children can use headsets to listen to taped stories. Provide a private spot such as an oversized carton for children to crawl inside and read. Include story props, such as a felt board and story characters, and stuffed animals that relate to book titles—a rabbit, for instance, next to a copy of *Mr. Rabbit and the Lovely Present* (Zolotow, 1962).

WRITING CENTER.   The writing center is usually next to the library corner. It requires a table and chairs, plus colored felt markers, crayons, pencils, and unlined paper in a variety of sizes and colors. Let children collect the work they do here in their own writing folders that can be stored in the writing center. A computer is important and a tape recorder is invaluable for story dictation when the teacher is not available (Morrow, 1997b).

Materials for making books are essential, including paper, hole punch, stapler, and construction paper. Blank books keyed to themes prepared by the teacher invite children to write. A bulletin board for children to display selected pieces of their writing is important, as well as a message board used to exchange notes among members of the class and the teacher. Mailboxes, stationery, envelopes, and stamps for children's incoming and outgoing mail may be placed in the writing center.

Integrating Literacy Materials Into the Content Areas

The teacher who is dedicated to the development of literacy throughout the curriculum is like a classroom architect, designing a learning environment that supports specific instructional strategies. Preparing a classroom for optimum literacy development includes not only instructional strategies, but also environmental planning, through the design of space and the selection and placement of materials in all content areas. As described in Chapter 7, programs that motivate early literacy development include an integrated approach to literacy learning. Books to read, materials to write with, things to listen to, and activities to talk about are incorporated into subject-area teaching. Literacy activities have more meaning when integrated into content areas (Dewey, 1966). Content themes encourage use of new vocabulary and ideas and provide a reason for reading and writing. With each theme studied, new books, posters, music, art projects, dramatic-play materials, and scientific objects are added.

When materials and activities for reading, writing, and oral language are incorporated into subject-area teaching, those content areas become a source for literacy development. Each thematic unit of study brings new opportunities to enhance literacy. Centers must have materials appropriate for their content, but one can always add materials that will encourage reading and writing. The following are examples of centers of learning and appropriate materials for kindergarten. In addition during a unit on animals, Ms. Roberts, one of the kindergarten teachers in our staff-development group, added additional materials that would stimulate reading and writing.

Art Center

GENERAL CENTER MATERIALS.   The materials usually found in the art center were easels, watercolors, brushes, colored pencils, crayons, felt-tipped markers, various kinds of paper, scissors, paste, pipe cleaners, scraps of fabric, wool, string, clay, play dough, food and detergent boxes for sculptures, books about artists, and books with directions for crafts.

MATERIALS FOR THE ANIMAL UNIT.   Directions for making play dough were written on a chart for the art center. After following these directions, children created real or imaginary animals for a pretend zoo they designed in the block area. As they entered the zoo the animals were given names that were written on index cards.

Music Center

GENERAL CENTER MATERIALS.   Permanent materials included a piano, a tape recorder with musical tapes, rhythm instruments, songbooks, and photocopies of sheet music for songs sung in class.

MATERIALS FOR THE ANIMAL UNIT.   Songs were sung about animals, and to promote literacy the words to new songs were written on chart paper and displayed in the area. Children were encouraged to read or copy the charts.

Math Center

GENERAL CENTER MATERIALS. Math center materials included scales, rulers, measuring cups, movable clocks, a stopwatch, a calendar, play money, a cash register, a calculator, dominoes, an abacus, a number-line, a height chart, an hourglass, numbers (felt, wood, and magnetic), fraction puzzles, geometric shapes, math workbooks, children's literature about numbers and mathematics, writing material for creating stories, and books related to math.

MATERIALS FOR THE ANIMAL UNIT. Counting books that feature animals such as *One, Two, Three: An Animal Counting Book* (Brown, 1976) or *One, Two, Three to the Zoo* (Carle, 1968) were placed in the math center.

Science Center

GENERAL CENTER MATERIALS. Materials typically found in the science center included an aquarium, a terrarium, plants, a magnifying glass, a class pet, magnets, a thermometer, a compass, a prism, shells, rock collections, a stethoscope, a kaleidoscope, a microscope, informational books and children's literature reflecting topics being studied, and blank journals for recording observations of experiments and scientific projects.

MATERIALS FOR THE ANIMAL UNIT. Ms. Roberts borrowed a setting hen whose eggs were ready to hatch and the class discussed the care of the hen. The students started an experience chart when the hen arrived and added to it daily, recording the hen's behavior and the hatching of the eggs. They listed new vocabulary words on a wall chart and placed books about hens in the science area. Children kept journals of events concerning the hen. There were index cards in the center for children to record new Very-own words relating to the hen.

Social Studies Center

GENERAL CENTER MATERIALS. The social studies center was filled with maps, a globe, flags, pictures of community figures, traffic signs, articles and pictures about current events, artifacts from other countries, informational books and children's literature reflecting topics being studied, and writing materials to make class books or individual books about topics being studied.

MATERIALS FOR THE ANIMAL UNIT. Pictures of animals from different countries were placed in the social studies area along with a map highlighting animal origins. Children could match the animals to the appropriate place on the map. They also made their own books about animals around the world.

Dramatic Play

GENERAL CENTER MATERIALS. This center included dolls; a telephone; stuffed animals; a mirror; food cartons; plates; silverware; newspapers; magazines; books; a telephone book; a cookbook; note pads; cameras and a photo album; table and chairs; a broom; a dustpan; and child-size kitchen furniture such as a refrigerator, sink, ironing board, and storage shelves.

MATERIALS FOR THE ANIMAL UNIT. This area was designed as a pet store for the animal theme. Books and magazines about pets, as well as pamphlets about pet care were placed in the center and pet posters labeled with animals' names were hung on the walls. Other materials included an inventory sheet of the things in the pet store, a cash register, and bill forms and receipts. There were stuffed animals in boxes that were supposed to be cages for dogs, cats, or other animals; they were labeled with the type of animal in the box and its name.

Block-Play Center

GENERAL CENTER MATERIALS. The block-play center contained blocks of many different sizes and shapes, figures of people and animals, toy cars and trucks, items related to themes being studied, paper and pencils to prepare signs and notes, and reading materials related to themes.

MATERIALS FOR THE ANIMAL UNIT. The block-play area became a zoo, housing animal figures, stuffed animals, and play-dough animals created by the children in the art center. Children used the blocks to create cages and made labels for each animal and section of the zoo such as *Petting Zoo, Bird House, Pony Rides, Don't Feed the Animals*, and

Don't Touch Us, We Bite. There were admission tickets and play money to purchase tickets and souvenirs.

Observations in a Literacy-Rich Classroom

Activities in the Literacy Center

When observing children engaged in activities during time in the literacy center, in a room prepared with a rich literacy environment as just described, the following was recorded.

In the library corner, Tim, Patty, and Donald were looking at books as they relaxed on soft pillows, all of them clutching stuffed animals under their arms. Ilene read to Todd in the box called the "private spot." Tasha and Allison used a felt board to tell the story of *The Three Billy Goats Gruff*. Tasha manipulated the characters and Allison told the story.

A group of children listened to a taped story of *The Little Red Hen* on headsets, tracking the print in the book as they listened. Each time they came to certain parts of the story they would chant aloud, saying, for example, "Not I," said the dog, "Not I," said the cat, "Not I," said the goat.

In the social studies center, John and Mark were making a book of animals from other countries, and in the science center Jan and Joanna were discussing how the new baby chicks looked and acted.

Content-Oriented Dramatic Play

The following observation from Ms. Roberts's kindergarten class illustrates how activities modeled by the teacher motivate reading and writing, when children use materials in social settings that have meaning, a function, and concept orientation.

In the dramatic-play area, which was designed as a veterinarian's office, children were reading to their pets in the waiting room while waiting for their turn with the doctor. The nurse was taking appointments on the telephone, and the doctor was examining a toy dog. After examining the dog, Preston, who was acting as the doctor, scribbled on the patient information form, and showed it to Geremy, the pet's owner, and said, "This says that you give your dog 10 pills with his dinner. He will feel better tomorrow. Keep him in bed with you, and be sure to give him lots of hugs."

With each thematic unit, Ms. Roberts helped her children design the dramatic-play center to reflect the topic being studied (see Figure 8 for additional ideas). When learning about animals, the students in her room decided to create this veterinarian's office. The class visited a veterinarian to help with their planning. They created the waiting room with chairs and a table filled with magazines and books in the dramatic-play center. Ms. Roberts suggested having pamphlets about good health practices for pets, which she had obtained from the veterinarian. The children made posters that listed the doctors' hours and said *No Smoking* and *Check in With the Nurse When You Arrive.* The nurse's table contained forms for patients to fill out, a telephone, telephone books, appointment cards, and a calendar. There were

Figure 8
Additional Ideas for Literacy-Enriched Thematic Play

In this chapter is a description of a veterinarian's office created to match the animal theme studied by the class. The area had been enriched by the addition of literacy materials to motivate reading and writing. Following are additional suggestions for the creation of areas for dramatic play to match other themes.

Theme: Nutrition—Create a restaurant, ice cream store, or bakery; include menus, order pads, cash registers, specials of the day, recipes, and lists of flavors or products.

Theme: Transportation—Create an airport with signs posting arrivals and departures, tickets, boarding passes, luggage tags, magazines and books for waiting areas, safety messages on the plane, and name tags for flight attendants.

Theme: Community Workers—Create a gas station and car repair shop. Toy cars and trucks can be used for props. There can be receipts for sales, road maps to help with directions to different destinations, repair manuals for fixing cars and trucks, posters that advertise automobile equipment, and empty cans of different products that are sold in stations (Morrow & Rand, 1991).

patient folders, prescription pads, white coats, masks, gloves, cotton swabs, a toy doctor's kit, and stuffed animals. Blank paper, a stapler, pencils, markers, colored pencils, and crayons were placed in the area as well. The classroom computer was relocated in the dramatic-play area for keeping patient records and other files. The center design was a collaborative effort by the teacher and children.

After preparing the environment with her students, Ms. Roberts modeled the use of the materials. She suggested, "While waiting for your turn to see the doctor, you can read to your pet and the nurse can ask you to fill out forms. The receptionist can talk to patients on the phone about problems with their pets, schedule appointments, and write out appointment cards. He or she can write bills, accept payments, and give receipts. The doctor can write prescriptions and patient reports." Later, Ms. Roberts joined the children in the dramatic-play area, pretending first to be the nurse, then the doctor, so that she could model the types of literacy behavior she hoped the children would try. Ms. Roberts was aware of the importance of the physical environment and social learning to help develop literacy skills by motivating children to communicate in varied ways.

Room designs like that in Ms. Roberts's classroom, which are filled with interesting, accessible materials and activities that are guided by the teacher, should develop literacy through positive and successful experiences. The social context allows for practicing skills, selecting activities, and taking responsibility for learning. These are all motivating elements that will help to ensure the development of lifelong voluntary readers who choose to read for pleasure and for information.

CHAPTER 9

Planning the Day: Organizing for Whole-Day and Half-Day Instruction

Scheduling the daily routine in kindergarten must take into account the social, emotional, physical, and intellectual level of the young children involved. It also must select the best from the models of early childhood theorists, such as Piaget, Froebel, Dewey, Montessori, the behaviorists, and Vygotsky. The environment should be prepared so that learning can take place naturally, but with the guidance and instruction that will help children achieve their fullest potential.

Young children cannot sit for long periods of time and must have a schedule that varies. Whole-class lessons that require sitting and listening should be limited in number and short in length, and should be followed by lessons that allow for movement. Quiet times should be followed by noisier periods. Children need large blocks of time for exploring the environment in play situations, using manipulative materials in learning centers, and spending time outdoors to learn. Children also need to have periods of instruction in small groups and on a one-to-one basis to cater to individual needs and interests. To nurture literacy, the teacher must allow for rich literacy experiences throughout the day, experiences using and enjoying language in all its forms and functions.

In scheduling the school day, teachers should include whole-class, small-group, and one-to-one settings for learning. There need to be teacher-directed experiences as well as activities in which children participate independently. Children should have opportunities for a variety of reading and writing experiences including oral reading and response experiences, silent reading from books and from their own writing, shared reading and writing, independent and collaborative reading and writing, guided reading and writing, reading and writing connected to content areas, performance of completed reading and writing activities, and assessment of progress.

Activities that develop literacy must be scheduled throughout the daily plan. On a daily basis children should have the opportunity to use and listen to oral language, to listen to storybook reading, and to respond to literature in various ways (this could be in writing, through acting out stories, through participating in the story reading, or through the use of flannel board stories). Children should be involved in independent reading and collaborative literacy experiences, and have some exposure to written language, either through observing the teacher's model or doing some writing themselves in the form of copying, tracing, or inventing. Literacy experiences should be integrated throughout the school day in all content areas, and children should be exposed to literacy learning in guided explicit lessons in small groups or on an individual basis.

This chapter provides sample outlines for whole-day and half-day kindergarten programs. We provide outlines for the school day as well as schedules including detailed dialogue. We begin with a whole-day program for kindergarten and then discuss a half-day program. We then offer a detailed outline that illustrates how literacy development and content-area instruction can be integrated throughout a school day. Please note that elements of the literacy framework and thematic framework are included throughout the school day. They include all the language arts: reading, writing, listening, speaking, and viewing. They also include all of the literacy experiences suggested in Chapters 6 and 7 such as oral reading and response to literature, shared writing and reading, guided reading and writing, independent and collaborative reading and writing, content-area connections in literacy activities, performance of activities accomplished, and assessment of completed experiences.

Outline for a Whole-Day Kindergarten Program

8:30 TO 9:00: CHILDREN ARRIVE AT SCHOOL WITH QUIET ACTIVITIES
1. Select a book to read.
2. Copy a journal entry that is written on the board.

9:00 TO 9:45: MORNING GATHERING ON RUG IN THE LITERACY CENTER

1. Review the calendar, weather, and attendance.
2. Minilesson in social studies or science.
3. Oral language development: Five children discuss and share something brought from home related to the theme being studied.
4. Writing the morning message (shared writing and reading): Children dictate a chart, the teacher writes it, they read it back. Class members look for letters they have been discussing and circle them. They then generate a list of words beginning with those letters.
5. After the morning-message lesson, children do a stretching exercise or sing a song because they have been sitting for a while.
6. Read aloud and responses: interactive story event.
7. Review of independent activities to take place during guided reading and writing instruction.
   a. Select a book for buddy reading.
   b. Write or draw a new ending to a story.
   c. Use word-analysis skills materials in the literacy center.
   d. Theme-related activities are at several centers.

9:45 TO 10:30: GUIDED READING AND WRITING AND INDEPENDENT WORK

1. Independent work begins.
2. Guided reading and writing lesson.
   a. Children review something they know well, such as narrating a familiar storybook related to the theme.
   b. Sentence strips are cut for the book and children match strips to sentences in the book.
   c. Children are asked to write a word or sentence about what they like best in the story. They can draw or copy.
   d. A word-analysis lesson occurs related to skills emphasized in the morning message.
   e. A new book is introduced. The group talks about the pictures in the story to predict what it will be about.
   f. The teacher reads the story to the children. The children read the story with the teacher.
   g. Each child's progress is recorded and a note is sent home about progress and homework.
3. Individual Conferences

Teachers also may hold individual conference for special needs and to assess student progress. Conferences last about 5 minutes or less per child.

10:30 TO 10:45: SNACK

10:45 TO 11:15: WHOLE-CLASS MATH LESSON

The teacher does a lesson from the math curriculum for the entire class. After assigning independent work, she meets with groups for individual needs and to differentiate instruction.

11:15 TO 11:50: FREE-CHOICE PERIOD

All centers may be used and have special projects related to the social studies or science theme.

11:50 TO 12:00: CLEAN UP FOR LUNCH

12:00 TO 1:15: LUNCH AND OUTDOOR PLAY

1:15 TO 1:40: LITERACY-CENTER TIME

Children use materials in the literacy center, library corner, and writing center.

1:40 TO 2:00: WHOLE-GROUP LESSON IN SCIENCE, SOCIAL STUDIES, ART, MUSIC, MATH, OR LANGUAGE ARTS

A different lesson in one of these content areas can take place daily.

2:00 TO 2:30: CENTER TIME FOR SPECIAL PROJECTS

During this center time only the literacy, math, science, and social studies centers are open and each has a special project.

2:30 TO 2:50: CIRCLE TIME, PERFORMANCE OF TASKS COMPLETED, AND REVIEW OF THE DAY

Five children who have finished an activity are asked to share their experiences. The activities of the day are reviewed.

2:50 TO 3:00: GET READY TO GO HOME AND DISMISSAL

A Half-Day Program for Kindergarten

With the shorter time in a half-day program the amount of time for each part of the day is cut. Where several groups may be seen during guided reading in the whole-day program, fewer can be seen in a day in the half-day program. Fewer children can share accomplishments or things brought from home in a given day, and whole-group lessons will alternate more, with less occurring in each content area. Although all of the same activities can occur, they occur less frequently and for shorter periods of time.

8:30 TO 8:45: CHILDREN ARRIVE AT SCHOOL WITH QUIET ACTIVITIES
1. Select a book to read.
2. Copy a journal entry that is written on the board.

8:45 TO 9:20: MORNING GATHERING ON RUG IN THE LITERACY CENTER
1. Review the calendar, weather, and attendance.
2. Minilesson in social studies or science.
3. Oral language development: Five children discuss and share something brought from home related to the theme being studied.
4. Writing the morning message (shared writing and reading): Children dictate a chart, the teacher writes it, they read it back. Class members look for letters they have been discussing and circle them. They then generate a list of words beginning with these letters.
5. After the morning-message lesson, children do a stretching exercise or sing a song because they have been sitting for a while.
6. Read aloud and responses: Interactive story event.
7. Review of independent activities to take place during guided reading and writing instruction.
   a. Select a book for buddy reading.
   b. Write or draw a new ending to a story.
   c. Use word-analysis skills materials in the literacy center.
   d. Theme-related activities are at several centers.

9:20 TO 9:50: GUIDED READING AND WRITING AND INDEPENDENT WORK
1. Independent work begins.
2. Guided reading and writing lesson.
   a. Children review something they know well, such as narrating a familiar storybook related to the theme.
   b. Sentence strips are cut for the book and children match strips to sentences in the book.
   c. Children are asked to write a word or sentence about what they like best in the story. They can draw or copy.
   d. A word-analysis lesson occurs related to skills emphasized in the morning message.

      e. A new book is introduced. The group talks about the pictures in the story to predict what it will be about.

      f. The teacher reads the story to the children. The children read the story with the teacher.

      g. Each child's progress is recorded and a note is sent home about progress and homework.

   3. Individual conferences: Teachers also may hold individual conference for special needs and to assess progress. Conferences last about 5 minutes or less per child.

9:50 TO 10:00: SNACK

10:00 TO 10:30: WHOLE-CLASS MATH LESSON

The teacher does a lesson from the math curriculum for the entire class. After assigning independent work, she meets with groups for individual needs and to differentiate instruction.

10:30 TO 11:00: FREE-CHOICE PERIOD

Two days a week all centers including art, music, dramatic play, and the block area may be used and children have complete free choice of activities. One day a week only four centers are open because there are special activities at the social studies, science, math, and literacy centers. Two days a week are set aside just for literacy-center time.

11:00 TO 11:25: WHOLE-GROUP LESSON IN SCIENCE, SOCIAL STUDIES, ART, MUSIC, MATH, OR LANGUAGE ARTS

A different lesson in one of these content areas can take place daily.

11:25 TO 11:50: OUTDOOR PLAY OR GYM DEPENDING ON THE WEATHER, OR CIRCLE TIME, PERFORMANCE OF TASKS COMPLETED, OR REVIEW OF THE DAY

Outdoor play and gym end the day, alternating with circle time to discuss completed tasks and to review the day.

11:50 TO 12:00: GET READY TO GO HOME AND DISMISSAL

A Script for a Whole-Day Kindergarten Program

The following plan is scripted to illustrate how literacy development and content-area instruction can be integrated throughout a whole-day kindergarten program. To do this we will assume that the topic under study is animals. The teacher has prepared the environment to encourage reading, writing, and discussion about the topic with a variety of materials.

Books about animals that are found in the zoo, on the farm, as pets, and in the woods are featured on the open-faced bookshelves in the literacy center. The science and social studies table has collections of pictures and figures of the four different types of animals, with farm animals and animals in the woods featured in these centers. Pets and zoo animals are featured in the block-play and dramatic-play areas. The classroom should include some animals, such as gerbils, hamsters, guinea pigs, newts, hermit crabs, an aquarium of fish, or a rabbit. These will be placed near the dramatic-play area because it is designed as a veterinarian's office. The teacher has borrowed a hen that is sitting on her eggs waiting for them to hatch. In the block-play area there is a toy barn, a silo, animal figures, and farm equipment to encourage interesting play that will create language. Index cards are present for labeling animals and making signs such as *Deer Crossing* or *No Hunting*.

8:30 TO 9:00: CHILDREN ARRIVE AT SCHOOL WITH QUIET ACTIVITIES

Children arrive at school, put outdoor clothing away, and proceed with daily quiet activities. Children can work alone or in collaboration with one another.

1. Select a book to read from the open-faced bookshelves, alone or with a partner, related to the theme being studied.
2. Copy a journal entry that is written on the board, such as the date, a word for the day, a short message, or a picture. Children can write in whatever fashion they are able.

9:00 TO 9:45: MORNING GATHERING ON RUG IN THE LITERACY CENTER

1. Review the calendar, weather, and attendance.
2. Minilesson in social studies or science related to the theme being studied as follows: The teacher asks the children to think of and name all the farm animals they can. She makes a list of the animals as they are named and then asks the reason each of the animals is on the farm. For example cows are on the farm to give milk and chickens are there to lay eggs; these products are sold by the farmer so we have food to eat. The products

mentioned are written next to each animal's name with a picture. Children are encouraged to copy the list in their journals and copy words they like on their Very-own word card.

3. Oral language development: Five children are given the opportunity to discuss and share something brought from home related to the theme being studied. Each day there are five children who have this opportunity. They talk to the class about what it is they have brought and how it relates to what the are studying. They are to speak in complete sentences.

4. Writing the morning message (shared writing and reading):
   a. Children dictate the message that reflects a topic that the teacher suggests. Usually it is related to the topic being studied. In this case the children had just visited the zoo and they were to dictate what they saw. The teacher writes what is said on large chart paper.
   b. The class reads the message together as the teacher tracks the print with a pointer.
   c. At the bottom of the chart the teacher has written the letters *Pp* and *Bb* that are being studied along with the unit about animals because they appear often in the theme. Children are asked to come up to the chart and circle any *P*s or *B*s they may see. Afterward they generate a list of words beginning with *P* and *B*.

The text on the chart reads as follows:

Our Trip to the Zoo

Our class took a trip to the zoo.
We got to pet some animals in the petting zoo.
There were goats, bunnies, pigs, and sheep there.
We saw some big wild animals too.
We saw a big brown bear, a tiger, and a giraffe.
We saw beautiful birds. There was a peacock,
and a flamingo, and a parrot.
The zoo was fun. We want to go again.

After this lesson, children do a stretching exercise or sing a song related to the theme, because they have been sitting for a while. A song related to the discussion would be "Old MacDonald Had a Farm" or "The Farmer in the Dell." It is a good idea for the class to move to another portion of the room for storytime so it always has a designated spot and so children are able to stretch and move around.

5. Read aloud and responses:
    a. The selected book relates to the theme being studied.
    b. Before reading, the teacher sets a purpose: He or she builds background for the story, incorporates a strategy for students to learn such as K-W-L, and tells students to think about an activity they will do after the reading related to the text.
    c. During storybook reading, the teacher allows for reactions, discussion, or chanting of text if desired.
    d. After the story is read, the teacher discusses it in light of the designated purpose set at the beginning and the activity the students will be doing.

The teacher has selected the story *The Little Red Hen*, a farm-animal story, for the shared book reading experience. He or she will tell the story using felt figures on a felt board and ask the children to participate in the parts where the animals respond, "Not I." After telling the story the teacher uses a Big Book to review the pages and point out the words "Not I." Before finishing the storybook reading he or she asks the children if they think the little red hen was right in not letting the animals share the bread, and if there were other ideas for the ending of the story. The teacher then leads the children into independent reading and writing activities to take place during guided reading.

6. Review of independent activities during guided reading and writing instruction:
    a. The teacher selects a theme-related book for buddy reading. Students take turns reading the book and discussing it.
    b. Students write or draw a new ending to the story of *The Little Red Hen*. The Big Book and the felt figures for the story will be in the literacy center to use as well. Students discuss what they are thinking about writing with a partner before proceeding. They share their work with their partner after finishing.
    c. The literacy center has some work related to the word-analysis skills being learned, which are modeled by the teacher. There are sheets of paper with the letters *Pp* and *Bb* on them. Children are to find objects in the room that begin with these letters and write them on the paper.

d. There are activities at the art, math, and literacy centers that can be done after items a, b, and c listed earlier.

Art Center: Create animals out of play dough. On a 3 × 5 card name the type of animal you made and where it comes from (such as the farm, woodland, or zoo), and give the animal a name.

Math Center: Paper has been divided into four parts and labeled zoo animals, pets, farm animals, and woodland animals. Children are to walk around the classroom and write the names of animals they find in pictures or figures and classify them in the boxes where they belong. When each box is full, count how many animals are in each box and how many animals were found altogether. Put the numbers on the lines provided in the boxes and for the total.

9:45 TO 10:30: GUIDED READING AND WRITING AND INDEPENDENT WORK

There are five teams of children. The teacher will meet with at least three during guided reading instruction. She also might meet with individual children for conferences for special needs. The rest of the children participate in self-directed activities modeled by the teacher at the centers.

The teacher meets with each team. He or she keeps records about student performance and assigns homework. The child is given a note to take home to his or her parent about the work to be done with the parent. The note is to come back signed.

Children come prepared with their book in a bag, which includes all materials on which they are working, such as a writing journal, reading book, and letters of the alphabet.

1. Guided reading and writing lesson

   a. Children review something they know well, such as narrating a familiar storybook related to the theme. The book is discussed to determine what children liked best.

   b. Sentence strips are cut for the book and children match strips to sentences in the book.

   c. Children are asked to write a word or sentence about what they like best in the story. The children copy a word or sentence from the book or write it themselves if they are able.

   d. A word-analysis lesson occurs related to skills emphasized in the morning message, which includes the initial sound-symbol relation of the letters *Bb* and *Pp*. A new letter is introduced.

e. A new theme-related book is introduced. The group talks about the pictures throughout the story and predicts what it will be about. The teacher gives each child words from the book to add to his or her list of new words. They say the words and the teacher asks how many sounds they hear in the word. They make the sounds in the word and then blend them together.

f. The teacher reads the story to the children. The children then read the story with the teacher.

g. Progress for each child is recorded and a note is sent home about progress and homework.

2. Individual conferences

Teachers also may hold individual conferences for children with very special needs. These last about 5 minutes or less per child. Work is tailored to individual needs, interests, and ability level. The following are examples of three different conferences.

Child A: Darren has had little experience with books prior to coming to school; therefore the teacher tries to provide him with those experiences that many children already have had. The teacher continues with discussion concerning concepts about print that she began at the last conference, such as where the print is on the page and which are the pictures. She will use a book that is familiar to the child and that she has read to him before. They will talk about where the front and the back of the book are. The teacher then will read the story, occasionally asking the child to point out the print on the page and then the picture, or ask where to start reading on this new page. For the contract assignment, she asks Darren to look at many books and find the beginning and the end, the print that is to be read, and the picture. Before Darren leaves the teacher asks if the child would like a new word he heard in the story for his Very-own word collection. The teacher will write it down for him on a 3 × 5 card.

Child B: Jim has had substantial experiences with books and is beginning to merge narrational reading and conventional reading of print. He has shown an interest in words and asks to have them identified. He also is interested in associating letters and sounds to help him become a more independent reader.

The teacher selects a familiar story (*Are You My Mother* [Eastman, 1990]) and asks Jim to read it. He uses book-reading intonation and looks at the print as he narrates the story. In particularly predictable parts, Jim begins to attend to the print and the teacher encourages this behavior by asking him to find the words "Are you my mother?" every time they are said by an animal in the story. When Jim is finished reading the story the teacher asks, "If you were the baby bird, would you have looked for your mother or just waited for her? And why?" For a contract assignment, the teacher asks Jim to read three familiar storybooks and write down all the words he finds that he can read during attempted story readings. Before Jim leaves, he is asked if he would like a new word for his Very-own word collection.

Child C: Jennifer has had little experience with writing material at home and is reluctant to try to write. The teacher begins with a discussion of Jennifer's family; the teacher is aware that a new baby has just arrived. The baby's name is Joseph, and the teacher asks Jennifer if she will write something about her new brother. Jennifer responds that she cannot write. The teacher explains that she does not have to write like an adult but that children can write in their own way, showing her samples of other children's writing that include invented spelling, random letters, and scribble writing. The teacher asks Jennifer to try as the other children have and then asks Jennifer what she would like to write about her brother. Jennifer responds that she would like to write his name but she cannot. Because the child is so reluctant the teacher writes the name *Joseph* on a 3 × 5 card and asks Jennifer if she can copy some of it. Jennifer copies the *J* and comments that is the first letter of her name too. The teacher asks Jennifer to draw a picture of her new brother for her contract activity and to think of what she would like to say about him and try to write it in her own way for next time. The word *Joseph* becomes Jennifer's new Very-own word.

10:30 TO 10:45: SNACK

A child who is in charge puts on a tape that indicates it is time for snack. The tape often will have a song related to the theme or be a narrated story about the theme. The snack also is related to the theme, for example animal crackers with bug juice. Children are encouraged to discuss the animal cracker they are eating.

10:45 TO 11:15: WHOLE-CLASS MATH LESSON

The teacher does a lesson from the math curriculum for the entire class and gives them activities to carry out. While they are working on a skill sheet and other cooperative activities, she meets with groups to accommodate individual needs and to differentiate instruction based on development of math skills. The teacher has three math groups and sees one each day. Children can use the math center materials after they have finished assigned work from the whole-group lesson, and an assignment they have for their math group which they can work on together.

11:15 TO 11:50: FREE-CHOICE PERIOD

All centers may be used and all are available for use. There may be a special art project set up in the art center each week for small groups of children, or food preparation related to the theme. Items are added to the areas that incorporate the animal theme and encourage exposure to print.

Dramatic Play: As described in Chapter 8, this has been set up as a veterinarian's office.

Art Center: Provide a simple recipe for play dough on an experience chart with materials laid out, for example:

How to Make Play Dough
Put 2 cups of flour into a bowl.
Add 1 cup of water.
Add 1 tablespoon of salt.
Add l teaspoon of food coloring of your choice.
Mix together with your hands until it feels like play dough.
Add more salt if it is too sticky.
Add 1 tablespoon of water if it is too dry.
Add 1 tablespoon of flour if it is too wet.

When the children have made their piece of play dough it should be shaped into an animal of their choice.

Five children work daily at the art center during free play to create their animal; oral language is encouraged as they follow the directions to make the play dough and discuss textures. Continued conversation will be generated as they create their animals. It is advisable that an adult be available for supervision.

Block Corner: Set up this area to be a zoo for the zoo component of the unit. Include tickets for admission, posters of zoo animals with their names on them, pamphlets about the zoo (from a real zoo), and pamphlets discussing zoo animals. Provide figures of zoo animals for children to use when they construct a zoo from the blocks. Typical signs such as the name of the zoo, *Don't Feed The Animals*, *I Bite*,

Petting Zoo, *Pony Rides*, and signs identifying animals in the block-corner zoo created by the children should be placed in the area.

Social Studies Center: As described earlier, this area is set up with materials that focus on farm animals and animals from the woods. The social studies section may have a small store for selling farm products, such as eggs, milk, vegetables, or wool from sheep. This area would include a road side sign saying *Fresh Farm Products*, an *Open* and *Closed* sign, a cash register, pads for adding and listing items purchased, signs for products being sold, food posters representing the items being sold, brown bags for packaging groceries, play money, and markers for pricing food.

Science Center: This area has the setting hen. Children are to keep a daily log about the progress of the hen's eggs. Each child is to find time during the day to check on the hen and record what is happening.

11:50 TO 12:00: CLEAN UP FOR LUNCH

12:00 TO 1:15: LUNCH AND OUTDOOR PLAY

After lunch children play outdoors if weather permits. If not, they play in the gym for the purpose of participating in large motor activities.

The outdoor play should continue the unit topic being studied. Allow part of the outside play area to be turned into a farm where seeds can be planted and vegetables grown. Markers can be placed to identify what is being grown, and signs put up that say *Careful Don't Step on the Plants*.

1:15 TO 1:40: LITERACY-CENTER TIME

Children use materials in the literacy center, which includes the library corner and writing center. They read books, listen to books from taped stories, tell and write stories, create literature manipulatives for literacy props such as felt-board stories, roll stories, and music stories.

Added to the materials already in the literacy center, and featured on the open-faced bookshelves, are several books dealing with farm animals, zoo animals, pets, and animals found in the woods. Animal stories have been taped to listen to on the headsets and animal puppets are placed in the oral language center for storytelling. Added to the writing center are animal pictures to write about, word lists about animals to copy, empty booklets for children to create animal books, and paper cut in the shape of animals on which to write stories. Animal puzzles, labeled pictures of animals to alphabetize, animal lotto, animal dominos, a concentration animal card game, and animal sewing cards are placed with the language arts manipulatives.

During this period children can participate in any of the literacy center activities. They are encouraged to look at at least one book during the time period and at least three times a week they are encouraged to do some writing at the writing center. The special writing projects for this week are to make an animal book about a pet, zoo animals, farm animals, animals in the woods, or a combination book including all types of animals. Children are encouraged to use their Very-own words during this period and to ask for new ones if they have requests.

1:40 TO 2:00: WHOLE-GROUP LESSON IN SCIENCE, SOCIAL STUDIES, ART, MUSIC, MATH, OR LANGUAGE ARTS. A DIFFERENT LESSON IN ONE OF THESE CONTENT AREAS CAN TAKE PLACE DAILY, DEPENDING ON THE NEED. THE SAMPLE LESSON PROVIDED HERE IS A SOCIAL STUDIES LESSON

The class will discuss their trip to the farm. They will make a list of things to remember when going on the trip such as how to behave, safety rules, things they must bring such as spending money and lunch, what animal they are interested in seeing the most, what other things they would like to see or do when they are there, and what questions they have for the farmer. This list is recorded on an experience chart. Each child will be encouraged to write down one question for the farmer accompanied by a picture that will be sent to him in advance so he will know what to talk about when they get to the farm. Children sit down and write their questions and draw their pictures. The teacher acts as a model, aide, and guide in helping children with their work.

2:00 TO 2:30: CENTER TIME FOR SPECIAL PROJECTS

During this center time the literacy, science, social studies, and math centers are the only ones open. At the science center a special project has been set up dealing with making or churning butter. If it is possible to have a churn then children can churn milk into butter. If not, children can make butter by following a simple recipe posted in the science center with all the materials on hand. Six children are assigned to the center daily and an adult will supervise.

Recipe for Making Butter
Two children work together.
Take one baby food jar.
Fill it half way with whipping cream.

Place the lid on the jar tightly.
Take turns shaking the jar briskly for a total of 5 minutes.
Let stand for a few minutes and pour off the liquid.
Run cold water over the butter and pour off the water.
Add a little salt, spread on a cracker, and eat.

The teacher may choose to meet with small groups of children to help them with individual needs concerning some of the projects for the day, or on any of their particular needs. The teacher also may take this time to read to small groups of children.

2:30 TO 2:50: CIRCLE TIME, PERFORMANCE OF TASKS COMPLETED, REVIEW OF THE DAY

About five children who have finished an activity are asked to share their experiences with the rest of the class. This provides an audience for completed work. Over a period of a week each child will share some completed work.

The activities of the day are reviewed, with children telling things they liked or did not like and things they accomplished or still have to do.

A music activity involving large motor activity is appropriate with children listening to music and deciding what kind of animals the music makes them think of. They walk like elephants, jump like kangaroos, or waddle like ducks. A familiar song is *Go Tell Aunt Rhody*, with its words posted as the teacher points to the words as it is sung. This song is also a book that the teacher then reads at end the day.

2:50 TO 3:00: GET READY TO GO HOME AND DISMISSAL

Summary

This section of the book has presented a plan in early literacy development in kindergarten based on theory and research. The plan includes the preparation of a rich literacy environment. The activities include social interaction, peer interaction, and small-group and individual learning with guidance from an adult. The activities encourage literacy learning in a functional way with real-life experiences. They integrate them into all content areas to add enthusiasm, motivation, and meaning. There is careful monitoring in guided instruction, specifically in literacy, to enhance individual growth and there is ample space for children to learn through play, manipulation, and exploration.

Afterword

We began with a study to determine if there would be a difference in literacy achievement between children who attended half-day kindergarten and those who were in school all day. We also were interested in the nature of the literacy activities and time spent on the activities in these programs.

The results of the data were in favor of the whole-day programs, with whole-day children scoring significantly better on measures of reading and writing than those in half-day programs. Children in these programs also spent more time with literacy activities than children in the half-day kindergarten, although activities in each setting were similar. The quality of the instruction in both settings seemed to be equal, but the extra time did make a difference. The results of this investigation support the views of the National Association for the Education of Young Children in that the kindergarten curriculum designed by the administrators and teachers in the district where the study took place was based on developmentally appropriate practices with concern for the social, emotional, physical, and intellectual growth of the children. Objectives for instruction followed emergent literacy perspectives and the integrated language arts approach to literacy instruction. With this type of program implemented in whole-day and half-day kindergarten, the longer day proved to be better.

The observational data helped to support the results of the literacy achievement data. Although the half-day and whole-day teachers initiated literacy activities in the same categories of Storybook Reading, Knowledge About Print, Comprehension Strategies, Writing Activities, Oral Language Activities, and Literacy Integrated Into Content Areas, because there was more time in the school day the whole-day programs spent more time engaged in these experiences. Teachers also were able to implement additional activities and had more time to model and scaffold for children in these areas of literacy instruction.

From the data, from our knowledge of past research, and from our own investigations about early literacy development, we were able to construct a framework for literacy instruction, which constitutes the second portion of the book. We described objectives for early literacy instruction, and then types of experiences and structures in which to learn these objectives. Our intent was to provide for both the researcher and practitioner information that would be useful for the type of work they each do, and to illustrate how important and easy it is to blend the two together.

Early literacy development is of great concern at this time. Emphasis is being placed on appropriate practice. We do know that if we can help children to be successful with literacy development early in their lives, they are likely to remain successful thereafter. We hope that our investigation and practical application of the research adds some new information to the body of knowledge that already exists.

APPENDIX A

Incorporating a Unit on Nutrition

Why Is Food Important?

All people need food to eat and water to drink in order to live. Food and water are also necessary for animals and most plants to live. Food is important because it gives us the energy, strength, and nutrients we need to grow, work, and play.

What Are the Four Food Groups?

There are many types of food. Eating properly, along with plenty of sleep and exercise, will keep a person's body healthy and strong. Foods are separated into four major groups, and eating a proper amount of each daily will help ensure good health. Foods are divided into the following categories:

1. *Vegetable-Fruit Group*: It is recommended that four servings be eaten daily from this group. Most vitamins and roughage are obtained from fruits and vegetables. A good diet should contain dark green and yellow vegetables and citrus fruits.

2. *Bread-Cereal Group*: This group includes breads, rolls, bagels, crackers, cereals such as oats and rice, and pastas. Carbohydrates, necessary for the energy to work and play, and fiber are the primary benefits of this group. Four daily servings are suggested.

3. *Meat-Poultry Group*: Also included in this group are fish, beans, nuts, and eggs. This group provides minerals and much

of the protein in a person's diet. Protein is essential for building and maintaining muscles and it is important for overall growth. Two servings are suggested daily.

4. *Milk-Cheese Group*: This group includes all dairy products, such as milk, cheese, yogurt, and cottage cheese. These products are also high in protein and contain nutrients that build strong bones and teeth. Many products in this group tend to have a high fat content. Three servings are the recommended daily intake.

A proper diet, including ample portions of these groups, is essential for a healthy, growing child. However, there are also foods known as "empty calorie foods" or "junk foods." These items provide no vitamins, minerals, or protein, and are not necessary for good health. Foods in this group include soda, candies, potato chips, and some seasonings and spices. On occasion these foods are fine in moderate doses, but a well-rounded diet containing items from the four major food groups is best.

What Are the Sources of Food?

Most of our food is grown on farms (from plants such as fruits and vegetables, and animals such as cows and poultry). Other foods we eat, like fish, come from rivers, lakes, and oceans. Many people are involved in the food process and work hard on farms to grow the food we eat, or on boats catching fish.

Most people purchase their food in supermarkets. Food can be bought either fresh, frozen, dried, canned, packaged, or processed. Some people also have small vegetable gardens in their backyards or flower boxes and grow foods such as tomatoes, string beans, cucumbers, and zucchini.

How Do People Prepare and Eat Food?

Different foods have different colors, tastes, textures, and odors. Our senses of taste and smell play a large part in what we like to eat. Foods can be eaten raw, cooked, or dried, and not all parts of all foods can be eaten. The flesh of fruit is eaten, but not the seed, and the skin of some fruits, like apples and grapes, is eaten, but the skin of others, such as bananas and oranges, is not. The leaves, stems, roots, or flowers of vegetables are eaten, but rarely is more than one part of the same vegetable used. Likewise, the meaty part of some animals is eaten, while the bones and fat sections are not.

Much of the food we eat is prepared in a kitchen. Some foods are specially prepared for people with diet restrictions, such as babies or those with allergies or physical handicaps. Special preparation can include strained or pureed foods or mildly-seasoned foods.

Food can be eaten in many ways such as drinking, using forks, spoons, chopsticks, or fingers. Foods we drink are called beverages.

People from different cultures eat different types of food. It is important to learn about and appreciate foods from different multicultural backgrounds.

Source: Flemming, B.M., Hamilton, D.S., & Hicks, J.D., (1977). *Resources for creative teaching in early childhood education.* New York: Harcourt, Brace Jovanovich.

Newsletter To Parents About Nutrition

Dear Parents:

Your child will be participating in a unit about nutrition. This unit will include the study of why food is important, the four food groups, sources of food, and how people of many cultures prepare food.

The nutrition unit will cover all subject areas—play, art, music, social studies, science, math, and literacy (reading, writing, listening, and oral language) that will be incorporated within the theme. Some of the exciting activities we do at school may be carried out at home with your child.

At School and at Home

ART.   Art can be a wonderful learning experience for your child. Your child will refine eye-hand coordination and visual discrimination skills, and will explore and experiment with different art materials as he or she engages in many different activities. At school we will be creating macaroni collages and abstract designs with egg shells. At home you can encourage your child to use his or her imagination by providing these and other food-related materials for art activities. Remember art is for exploring what can be done with different materials rather than copying an adult model.

SCIENCE. Science explorations will be related to meaningful aspects of your child's life. We will be making a fruit salad. In this activity the children will have the opportunity to listen, follow directions, and learn where the fruit comes from and how it is grown. Making something simple at home like fruit or lettuce salad or a peanut butter and jelly sandwich and involving your child in the preparation of foods using simple recipes and children's cookbooks will further extend listening skills at home. During cooking experiences children observe the changing forms of food.

LITERACY. The letters *B*, *D*, *F*, and *M*, associated with the words *Bread*, *Dairy*, *Fish*, and *Meat* are being highlighted throughout this unit. Please assist at home by labeling food items with appropriate letters or words that have these and other beginning sounds. Items such as coupons, supermarket sale signs, and other print may be pointed out when you are outside the home.

Please read stories, informational books, cookbooks, or poems related to nutrition to your child. Discuss magazine and newspaper advertisements of food. Reading to your child or having him or her read to you using illustrations or retelling a story are all fine literacy activities that are valuable and enjoyable. Some books with food themes that can be found in the library are the following:

The Magic School Bus Inside The Human Body (Cole, 1988).
Poem Stew (Cole, 1981).
Pancakes, Crackers and Pizza (Eberts, 1984).
The Lip-smackin', Joke-crackin' Cookbook for Kids (Chambers, 1974).

We Need Your Help

We would like your assistance with our multicultural food of the week or your favorite food at your home. If you are able to help prepare a snack one day and discuss it, please sign your name and the type of snack you would like to prepare on the attached sheet.

If you have any other materials at home related to our nutrition unit, such as empty food containers, boxes, plastic food, seeds, nuts, beans, or magazine pictures that we may use in our dramatic-play area, please have your child bring them to class.

Other Activities To Do With Your Child

Go to the supermarket together. Prepare a list beforehand of the food you need to purchase. Try to purchase foods from each food group. Plant watermelon, avocado, or carrot seeds at home. Keep a diary or record of their growth.

Make simple nutritious recipes at home, like fruit salad or lettuce salad to help our lessons in school carry over.

Child's Corner. Ask your child to write or draw about something he or she did in school or with you about nutrition.

Help your child keep a journal of food he or she eats each day. The journal can be written in a notebook, on a pad, or on pieces of paper stapled together like a book.

If you have questions about the unit, please contact me. If you have additional ideas for the unit, please share them with us.

Sincerely,

I would like to prepare the following snack during your nutrition unit: _____ Parent's Name: _____

Preparing the Classroom Environment for the Nutrition Unit

To begin the unit on nutrition prepare the room so that the theme is evident to those who enter. Begin with some things suggested below and continue to add as the unit progresses. Display environmental signs and labels about nutrition wherever possible. Feature colors that represent the nutrition unit such as white for dairy products, green for vegetables, and red and yellow for fruit.

1. *Dramatic Play.* Turn this center into various restaurants and add the following items: menus, receipts, order-taking slips, recipe cards, 3 × 5 blank cards, charts, cookbooks, baking utensils, prop foods, signs commonly seen in restaurants, a cash register, play money, food posters, cooking magazines, and waiter and waitress clothing.

2. *Block Area.* In order to create places that food comes from such as farms and supermarkets, the following items can be added: farm props (animals and plants), supermarket props (play foods, receipts, money, and bags), environmental print signs and posters displaying food information, as well as cards for making signs.

3. *Outdoor Play.* In order to play lemonade stand or any other food stand outside, the following items can be added: tables for stands, signs to represent stand information, play money, a cash register, receipts, recipe charts for directions, and paper and pencils.

4. *Music.* Various songs on nutritional topics can be added to this center such as "Chicken Soup With Rice." All tapes should be accompanied by the written lyrics posted on the wall. Props to act out the songs also may be motivating.

5. *Art.* Include play dough and poster of a play dough recipe to make play foods. Include cooking and health magazines; dry foods to make collages (macaroni, peas, seeds); fruits and vegetables for printing with paint; paints; and green, red, yellow, and white scraps that represent the nutrition colors.

6. *Science.* Materials for various nutrition projects may be added: planting equipment, recipes and the ingredients needed, foods to be classified into the four food groups, seed packages, and goods to be tasted. All of these should be accompanied with charts and journals to record ongoing progress. Informational books about food and nutrition should also be added.

7. *Social Studies.* Pictures of foods and the four food groups and maps that depict where certain foods are produced may be added to this center. Recipe books representing different cultures also may be added.

8. *Math.* Various foods can be used as counters, such as macaroni or hard candies. Counting books that contain foods and blank books to create their own number books also are needed.

9. *Literacy Center.*
   a. *Writing Center.* Materials needed include a recipe box to share favorite recipes, food-shaped blank books, and a message board on which to share nutrition unit events for the day.

b. *Library Corner.* Include cooking magazines, such as *Good Housekeeping*, pamphlets about good nutrition, and a collection of nutrition books from all literature genres. (See following list.)

Library Corner Book List With Suggested Activities

Chambers, W. (1974). *The Lip-smackin', Joke-crackin' Cookbook for Kids*. New York: Golden Press. (cookbook) Have students select a recipe from the book and make it in class.

Cole, J. (1988). *The Magic School Bus Inside the Human Body*. New York: Scholastic. (informational) Students can create a Big Book of how food travels through the body.

DePaola, T. (1978). *The Popcorn Book*. New York: Holiday House. (picture book) Children can make a chart of the popcorn recipe and then follow the directions in order to make the popcorn.

Hoban, R. (1976). *Bread and Jam for Frances*. New York: Harper & Row. (picture storybook) Have children make and eat bread and jam. Then create an experience chart by asking the students to list words they would use to describe how it tasted.

Hopkins, L.B. (1985). *Munching: Poems About Eating*. Boston, MA: Little, Brown. (poetry) Each child can write a poem that describes a food and it can be written on paper that is shaped like the food they are describing.

Hutchins, P. (1986). *The Doorbell Rang*. New York: Mulberry Books. (predictable book) Children can make their own small predictable books based on this story.

Krauss, R. (1945). *The Carrot Seed*. New York: Scholastic. (picture book) Children can make a felt-board story of the carrot seed. They also can have a carrot for a healthy treat.

McCloskey, R. (1948). *Blueberries for Sal*. New York: Penguin. (picture storybook) Children can make and eat a fruit salad that contains blueberries. Then they can make a class book that describes the steps in making fruit salad.

Sharmat, M. (1980). *Gregory the Terrible Eater*. New York: Scholastic. (picture book) Collect props of empty food containers that have environmental print on them to use to tell the story.

Westcott, N.B. (1981). *The Giant Vegetable Garden*. (picture story-book) Children could plant their own vegetable garden and label each section of vegetables, as well as keep a journal on plant growth.

Introductory Lesson: Morning Message

Objective:
Children will understand that print is functional because it relays a message. This written message provides for vocabulary development and sound-symbol association.

Activity:
Introduce the students to the nutrition unit by writing a message on the board to them about some of the interesting facts they will be learning during the unit. The message could be based on the four food groups and look something like this: "Today we are going to begin learning about nutrition and how to care for ourselves. One way to take care of ourselves is to eat healthy foods. There are four major food groups: Meat, Dairy, Breads, and Fruit-Vegetables." Several examples of foods in each group also should be listed. Read the message with the class using a pointer to track the print. Afterward discuss the content of the message as well as special words, letters, and sounds. Identify *M, D, B* and *F* as the letters we will learn in the unit and associate them with the words *Meat, Dairy, Bread*, and *Fish*. Allow children to add to the message. Do a morning message daily to inform students of new nutrition facts as well as any special events or questions that are related to the unit.

Concepts About Print

Objective 1:
Children will become aware that words are made up of separate sounds that are blended together.

Activity: Sort by Sound
Create a chart with three columns. At the top of each column, paste or draw a picture of a food item that begins with the sound you wish to introduce. Request that children classify cut-out pictures of food (from magazines or newspapers) in the appropriate columns on

the chart. Provide additional shoeboxes labeled with sounds so that children may continue to classify different foods on their own. Later this activity can be used with ending sounds and vowel sounds as well.

Objective 2:
Children will recognize that spoken words may be written down and read. Oral vocabulary and sight vocabulary will be increased as they discuss, see, and write their Very-own words.

Activity: Very-own Words
Before reading *The Old Lady Who Swallowed a Fly* discuss with the children why it is dangerous to eat inappropriate food. After reading the story, discuss food they should not eat. Then ask them to name foods they like that are good for them and the character in the story. Write each child's favorite food on a 3 × 5 index card to be stored in their Very-own word container.

Objective 3:
Student will read a chart with functional environmental print. He or she will increase sight vocabulary and will follow the directions on the chart.

Activity: Environmental Print
A helper chart will be made that lists jobs for students to perform. The chart should be located in a visible area and will relate directly to the unit. Jobs may include cafeteria monitor, reading the lunch menu, and helping with the daily snack.

Objective 4:
Students will be able to identify the featured letter in a featured word, story, or song. They will associate the sound-symbol relation of the letter and will copy the letter from a story chart.

Activity: Featured Letters
Display pictures of food associated with the featured letters *B-Bread, D-Dairy, F-Fish, M-Meat*. Simple stories and songs with words beginning with the featured letters also may be used; for example, *Fanny Fish has flippers that she flaps as she floats on the waves.* Emphasize the sound the letter makes in each word and have the children write the letter. Students may be encouraged to bring in items from home that begin with the featured letter. Pictures of items that begin with the letter also may be made and added to a class book. Do one letter at a time and repeat the activities suggested.

Objective 5:

By creating an alphabet book, the children will review many of the nutrition words they have learned in the unit. Children will demonstrate knowledge of letters, both vowels and consonants, and words that are identified with specific letters and sounds.

Activity: Nutrition Alphabet Book

An alphabet book will be made and photocopied for each child in the class. Each letter will relate to nutrition (that is, *A-apple, B-banana, C-carrot, D-donuts, E-eggs, F-fish*, and so forth) and a complete sentence will be written with each letter (I like _____). The students will read the letters, words, and sentences with the teacher and with one another.

Oral Language

Objective 1:

Children will be given the opportunity to speak in complete sentences and improve their listening skills.

Activity: Show and Tell

Have students bring in their favorite foods from home representing different cultural backgrounds. Display and discuss with the class.

Objective 2:

Children will understand the language of others when spoken to and be understood by others when they speak.

Activity: Describing Game

The class is divided into the four food groups. Each child brings in foods from their food group. Have students describe their food to the class without them seeing it. The class must then guess what the food is.

Objective 3:

Children will use appropriate vocabulary for their level of maturity when retelling a story.

Activity: Story Retelling

Read a story related to nutrition, such as *The Very Hungry Caterpillar*, and allow the class to retell the story using food props that are in the book.

Objective 4:

Children will have the opportunity to increase their language complexity through the use of adjectives.

Activity: Food-Group Webs

List the four food groups on a chart and list the foods that go into each group. Select one food from time to time, brainstorm words that describe it, and illustrate it graphically with a web. (See Food Web on page 141.)

Developing Positive Attitudes

Objective 1:

Children will develop positive attitudes toward reading through interaction in a well-designed literacy center.

Activity: The Library Corner

Provide books in the classroom library relating to nutrition, the four food groups, and multicultural foods. Provide hand-stick puppets, taped stories, felt stories, and roll movies. Include different genres of literature related to the theme of nutrition (realistic literature, fairy tales, poetry, informational books, magazines, and newspapers). For examples, see list on page 136.

Objective 2:

Children will be provided with an independent reading and writing period to engage them in different forms of literacy thus developing in them an appreciation for literature.

Activity: Independent Reading-Writing Period

Introduce any new materials added to the literacy center related to nutrition. Review with the children the activities that may be selected during this time, as well as the rules to follow. When children are engaged in reading and writing, circulate among them and work along with them.

Objective 3:

Children will experience enjoyable literature while predicting outcomes using the context of a story.

Activity: *Goldilocks and the Three Bears* Prop Story

Read *Goldilocks and the Three Bears* storybook to the children. Use props such as a girl doll, three stuffed bears, and cereal bowls to tell the story again to the class. Encourage participation by having children use their knowledge of rhyme and context. Place the props in the library corner for the children to use.

Food Web

From Lesley M. Morrow, *Literacy Development in the Early Years: Helping Children Read and Write* (2nd Edition). Copyright 1993 by Allyn & Bacon. Used with author's permission.

Objective 4:
Children will tell a story through the use of a storytelling technique (chalktalk).

Activity: *Mr. Rabbit and the Lovely Present* Chalktalk

Read *Mr. Rabbit and the Lovely Present* and discuss the food in the story. Now retell the story and draw the fruit in the story as you come to each part. Use colored chalk on the chalkboard. Encourage children to retell the story themselves.

Concepts About Books

Objective 1:
Children will differentiate print from pictures and know what books are for.

Activity: Big Book

Create a class Big Book that contains pictures and sentences about each child's favorite food. After the class completes the book, read it together.

Objective 2:
Children will know that an author writes the words to a story.
Activity: Authors

Read *The Gingerbread Boy* to the class. Discuss the author of the story and explain that the author is the person who writes the words in a story. Allow the students to become authors by writing their own gingerbread boy adventures.

Objective 3:
Children will know that an illustrator draws the pictures in a book.
Activity: Illustrators
Read *It Looked Like Spilt Milk* to the class. Discuss the illustrator of the story and allow the students to become illustrators by drawing their own picture of what they see when they look at a cloud. Create a class Big Book of all the pictures.

Objective 4:
Children will understand that print is read from left to right.
Activity: Poetry Reading
Display a poem such as "Peas Porridge Hot" about foods on a large chart and read with the class. Use a pointer to show them how print is read from left to right. Create a class poem and read it in the same manner.

Comprehension

Objective 1:
Children will learn about story structure by identifying story elements (setting, theme, plot episodes, and resolution).
Activity: Story Structure
The Carrot Seed by Crockett Johnson has been read to the children in the past to discuss the food included in the nutrition unit. Before reading the story a second time ask the children to try to remember the time that the story takes place, where the story takes place, and who the characters are. After reading have the children identify the three setting elements, time, place, and characters. Do the same thing on other days with other story elements such as the theme, plot episodes, and resolution.

Have the children prepare a roll movie with four headings: setting, theme, plot episodes, and resolution. Encourage them to draw pictures and include narrative for each of the four sections of the roll movie. Do one section of the movie at a time. Repeat with other stories.

Objective 2:

Children will identify details in a story through literal questions asked by the teacher and demonstrate literal knowledge by acting out a story using stick puppets.

Activity: Literal Activity

Before reading *The Little Red Hen* tell the children to remember the things the hen wanted help with when baking the bread. After reading the story, have the children dramatize the episodes with stick puppets of the animals and the hen.

Objective 3:

Children will express feelings, predict, generalize, and problem solve.

Activity: Critical Activities

The story of *The Little Red Hen* is repeated. Role play a talk show and have a child take the part of the host interviewing the animals in the story asking why they did not help the hen and what they think about the fact that she did not share the bread with them. Then interview the hen as well. With another story such as *Gregory the Terrible Eater* interview his parents to try and find out why his eating problem exists. With *Goldilocks and the Three Bears* interview the bears to find out how they felt about what Goldilocks did in their house.

Objective 4:

Children will be exposed to poetry and create a poem.

Activity: Webbing and Creating Poetry

Brainstorm characteristics of food such as an apple and provide a graphic presentation with a web. List the characteristics of the food by writing adjectives to describe it. Create a web on the chalkboard. Encourage children to assist in putting together a poem by using the information on the web. Write the poem on the chalkboard. Encourage children to read it with you, tracking print from left to right as you read. Rewrite the poem on chart paper to display. (See Web Example on page 144.)

Writing

Objective 1:

Students will communicate with one another through writing about nutrition. They will see and use functional writing.

Web Example

About Apples
Apples can be shiny
Apples can be crunchy
Apples taste good
Apples can be sour or sweet
Apples can be red

Activity: Notice Bulletin Board

A notice bulletin board with student and teacher sections will be prepared in the classroom. Children may display their work on the board, as well as leave and receive messages in their space. Students can share messages, such as what they had for lunch and what food group each item belonged to. They also may decorate their personal space by drawing pictures related to nutrition.

Objective 2:

Children will be introduced to journal writing as a form of written expression. They will have the opportunity to use writing to convey meaning about things they have learned in the unit. The students will become authors and illustrators.

Activity: Journal Writing

Green Eggs and Ham will be read to the class. The children will be told about journal writing, with an emphasis placed on them becoming authors and illustrators. As in the story, the children will be encouraged to write about a food they do or do not like. They also will write periodically about their experiences with the nutrition unit. Conventional or invented writing, scribbling, and pictures are acceptable entries.

Objective 3:

Students will participate in brainstorming, drafting, conferencing, editing, and revising. They will engage in brainstorming and use an experience chart as a prewriting activity. The students will learn that books are written by authors and that they, too, are authors.

Activity: Shaped Nutrition Books

Story webs will be made on writing process approach experience chart paper as students talk about different characteristics of nutritional items. Each child will be writing stories about nutrition and teacher conferencing will take place. Finished products will be placed in books shaped like the food they write about. Pictures, scribbling, conventional, or invented writing will be accepted. Books can be in the shape of many foods such as apples, strawberries, meat, fish, or slices of bread.

Objective 4:

Students will be introduced to letter writing. They will learn that writing is a form of meaningful communication and will be participating in this important type of communication.

Activity: Nutritional Mail Service

The students will write letters to one another about nutrition through an in-class mail service. The class as a whole will write to the U.S. Department of Agriculture or any type of food-related organization to request pamphlets about good nutrition.

Play

Objective 1:

Children will engage in problem solving in dramatic play related to a nutrition theme and use environmental print.

Activity: Dramatic Play: Health-Food Restaurant

Turn the dramatic-play area into a health-food restaurant by adding menus, cookbooks, recipe charts, receipts, and other signs that would appear in a restaurant.

Objective 2:

Block play will be enhanced with theme-related play to acquire new concepts and participate in reading and writing.

Activity: Block Play: Where We Get Food

Have children create block constructions of the places that our food comes from, such as farms and supermarkets. Provide labels and appropriate props for their construction.

Objective 3:
Children will follow written directions and use print in a functional manner in their outdoor play, which provides a real-life experience.
Activity: Outdoor Play: Lemonade Stand
Create a lemonade stand outside. Post signs about how to make lemonade and how much it costs. Allow children to write receipts and keep lists of who has bought lemonade.

Objective 4:
Children will expand their vocabulary that is related to nutrition and read environmental print during theme-related dramatic play.
Activity: Dramatic Play: World Dining
Create restaurants based on the ethnic make up of your class. Provide menus and food props to go along with each new restaurant, such as all the things needed for a Chinese or Italian restaurant.

Art

Objective 1:
Children will have the opportunity to be creative using unusual materials. They will develop eye-hand coordination, fine motor skills, and listening skills.
Activity: Egg Art
The poem "Humpty Dumpty" will be read to the class. The teacher will provide egg shells broken into small pieces to create a collage representing Humpty Dumpty's broken shell.

Objective 2:
The children will learn that parts of most vegetables can be used for print painting as they explore and experiment with these materials.
Activity: Vegetable Print Painting
Children will use vegetable printing with ink or tempera paint. The ends of discarded vegetables and fruits will be used for print painting. Children will discuss their pictures and describe how they made them. A discussion of conservation and recycling may be conducted.

Objective 3:

Children will gain an appreciation for creativity and ingenuity by designing pictures and jewelry based on different cultures. They also will increase visual discrimination and enrich vocabulary through observation and discussion.

Activity: Macaroni Art

Pictures using macaroni, beans, dried fruits, or seeds can be made. Jewelry also can be made by using macaroni and string. Macaroni can be dyed by placing it in food coloring and water for 3 minutes. A multicultural theme may be introduced by stressing the use and design of different objects (such as Mexican or Native American necklaces). Students will observe one another's work and describe their own work to the class.

Objective 4:

Children will develop fine motor skills and increase visual discrimination through creating a collage. Oral communication also will be enhanced through discussion of the shape, color, form, line, and texture of the pictures they use in their collage.

Activity: Food Collage

Each student will make a collage using magazine or book pictures of different cultures. Pictures of food can be placed in groups representing different cultural backgrounds. Children can describe and display their collages in the classroom and to visiting parents and guests.

Music

Objective 1:

Children will sing about food, increase listening skills, and track print from left to right while reading a familiar book or lyric and singing a song about food.

Activity: Chicken Soup

Present the book *Chicken Soup With Rice* by Maurice Sendak along with the cassette tape sung by Carole King. As you sing the song, encourage children to read highlighted or repeated words such as eating, chicken, or soup, and emphasize the months of the year for sight vocabulary reinforcement. Ask the children if they recall how chicken soup was eaten during each month. Encourage children to include their favorite words in their Very-own words container.

Objective 2:
Children will create lyrics for a song, increase listening skills, and recognize rhyming words by singing a song about food.

Activity: Singing Rhymes

Sing the song "On Top of Spaghetti" (sung to the tune of "Old Smoky") with the class. Have the words written on an experience chart, and track print from left to right. Encourage children to sing the second time. Highlight the rhyming words in a different color to assist in recall.

Objective 3:
Children will increase listening and refine large motor skills as they sing and act out a song about food.

Activity: "Oats, Peas, Beans" Song and Dance

Have words printed on experience chart paper. Sing song "Oats, Peas, Beans" demonstrating actions to be used and referring to a chart where the action may be written and drawn. Encourage children to join in the second time, modeling movements as they sing. Props, such as a hoe, may be used to further encourage the actions to the song.

Social Studies

Objective 1:
The students will be shown the importance of working together and sharing. They also will be exposed to different cultures. Children will improve oral and written communication through discussion of the story and sharing of home soup recipes.

Activity: Stone Soup

The story *Stone Soup* will be read to the class. After reading, children may discuss the story, highlighting the parts where the community members add what they have to the soup. Cultural variation could be included such as Chinese eggdrop soup, Mexican gazpacho soup, Jewish chicken noodle soup, or American vegetable soup. Children will write and talk about soups from their family or culture. Favorite recipes can be added to a class Big Book.

Objective 2:

Children will focus on the importance of helping and caring for others who are in need. Being careful of strangers should be addressed. Children will increase oral communication skills and will practice sharing through family photographs. How food is used in the story will be discussed.

Activity: Hansel and Gretel

The fairy tale *Hansel and Gretel* will be read to the class. After reading, the students can discuss how Hansel and Gretel help each other in the story. Note how food is used throughout the story. A discussion of families also can be held. The focus will be on the positive aspects that each unique person adds to the family unit. Students may bring in photographs of their families and a class photo album can be made.

Objective 3:

Children will be exposed to aspects of conflict and resolution. They will see how cooperation and communication are important in developing and maintaining friendships. Cooperation and friendship skills will be increased through role playing. It will be noted how food is the source of conflict.

Activity: *The Three Billy Goats Gruff*

Before reading, the children will be asked to listen for the problems and resolution in the story *The Three Billy Goats Gruff*. Point out how food is the source of conflict. After the story is read, the students will discuss the problems (that is, the goats needing grass to eat and how to get across the troll's bridge) and the resolution (that is, they became friends). The students then can take turns through role playing the story.

Objective 4:

Children will be exposed to the foods and customs of different countries. They will develop an appreciation for the differences and contribution of other people and cultures. Oral and written communication skills will be further developed.

Activity: Country of the Week

Classwork will focus on a Country of the Week. Customs, foods, and major contributions of each country will be highlighted. Children will discuss the differences and similarities among the countries, with an emphasis on foods and the healthiness of each. The students also may write about their favorite food from each country. Another food will be featured at snack time.

Science

Objective 1:
Children will observe changes that occur in the form of food and they follow directions in preparing a recipe.
Activity: Making Applesauce
Read *Johnny Appleseed* to the class. Discuss the nutritional value of apple products. Make applesauce with the class. Post the recipe and use it as a reference to point out all the steps involved in making applesauce.

Objective 2:
Children will hypothesize what will happen during the growth of a seed they plant. They will record their observations of the growth as it occurs.
Activity: Planting
Allow each student to plant a lima bean seed and keep the plants in the classroom. Have the students write entries in journals each day to record the progress of their plant's growth.

Objective 3:
Children will understand the connection of oral and written language as they observe and record the growth of a plant. They will summarize the growth process when it is complete.
Activity: Potato Growth
Have students place potatoes in clear plastic cups filled with water. Watch their growth daily and discuss and graph the progress of each student's project.

Objective 4:
Seeds and plants will be classified and labels read from seed packages and matched to one another.
Activity: Seed Exploring
Display many types of vegetable seed packets and their corresponding products. Allow students to attempt reading the packages and matching them with their correct products.

Math

Objective 1:
Children will follow oral directions as they compose a nutrition counting book. Children will count and write numbers to 10.

Activity: My Nutrition Counting Book

Explain to children that they will be authors and illustrators of their own nutrition counting book. Pass out copies of premade number books and review directions. Children will need to color illustrations of "how many" and trace the number on each page. Each page will feature a number with that amount of one food item represented.

Objective 2:
Children will relate pictures to text and see that pictures and print go together. Children will classify objects according to shape (triangles, circles, and squares).

Activity: Sort a Food

Read *Pancakes, Crackers and Pizza*, (Eberts, 1984) to the class. Emphasize the different shapes of food as you read. Create a chart with three columns (triangles, circles, and squares). Encourage children to classify cut-out pictures of food (from a magazine or newspaper) in the appropriate columns on the chart. Provide three shoeboxes labeled with each shape so that children may continue to classify different foods on their own.

Objective 3:
Children will practice counting to 12 and matching the correct number of items to the number of words.

Activity: Counting "Eggsactly"

Display an egg carton with number words printed on the bottom of each egg hole in the carton. Provide a variety of seeds, nuts, and beans for children to match to the correct amount by placing them in the egg holes.

Culminating Activity

Objective:
Share the products of the unit with parents and or other classes in the school.

Activities:

Prepare a nutritious food for a snack to share with guests.

Sing a song related to food from the unit.

Role play a story such as *The Little Red Hen*.

Show science plants and discuss how they grew.

Display art projects related to the unit and describe how they were made.

Assessment Measures From the Research Study

Directions for Observing the Teacher

You are to observe the teacher throughout the entire morning and those who teach in the afternoon sessions the whole day. Observations will be recorded at 20-minute intervals on the sheets provided (see pages 154 to 157). We do want you to write down all activities that happen, especially in literacy. Therefore, for each time slot listed, include the following:

1. Describe *what* literacy activity is going on.
2. Describe *materials* used by the teacher.
3. Describe *where* the activity takes place, *where* are the children, and *where* is the teacher.
4. Indicate if the activity is *teacher directed* (*TD*) or in an independent setting where the child is *independent of the teacher* (*IN*).
5. Indicate if the activity is *whole group* (*WG*), *small group* (*SG*), *one to one* (*1 TO 1*).

Sample Teacher Entry

9:20 to 9:40

What: Teacher read to children and encouraged discussion.

Materials: Big Book related to animal theme

Where: Teacher sat in a large chair, children sat on rug in the library corner.

TD or *IN*: The teacher directed the activity

WG, SG, 1 TO 1: WG activity

For all literacy activities observe and include information similar to what is written earlier.

When the activity is not literacy related simply identify what it was and the time slot, for example:

9:40 to 10:00

> *What*: Naptime
>
> *Materials*:
>
> *Where*:
>
> *TD* or *IN*:
>
> *WG, SG, 1 to 1*:

The what could be science, social studies, snack, outdoor play, music, art, or play. If it is play and the children engage in literacy activities, include what is happening.

When you finish writing your narratives try to fill in the sweep sheets based on the information you have collected.

Observation Sheet for Recording Literacy Activities in Half-Day Programs

Teacher Form

Teacher Name and ID #: _____

School _____ Half day–1, Whole day–2

9:00 to 9:20

> *What*:
>
> *Materials*:
>
> *Where*:
>
> *TD* or *IN*:
>
> *WG, SG, 1 TO 1*:

9:20 to 9:40

> *What*:
>
> *Materials*:
>
> *Where*:
>
> *TD* or *IN*:
>
> *WG, SG, 1 TO 1*:

(continued)

Observation Sheet for Recording Literacy Activities in Half-Day Programs (continued)

9:40 to 10:00
What:
Materials:
Where:
TD or *IN*:
WG, SG, 1 TO 1:

10:00 to 10:20
What:
Materials:
Where:
TD or *IN*:
WG, SG, 1 TO 1:

10:20 to 10:40
What:
Materials:
Where:
TD or *IN*:
WG, SG, 1 TO 1:

10:40 to 11:00
What:
Materials:
Where:
TD or *IN*:
WG, SG, 1 TO 1:

11:00 to 11:20
What:
Materials:
Where:
TD or *IN*:
WG, SG, 1 TO 1:

11:20 to 11:30
What:
Materials:
Where:
TD or *IN*:
WG, SG, 1 TO 1:

Observation Sheet for Recording Literacy Activities in Whole-Day Programs

Teacher Form

Afternoon Kindergarten

Teacher _____

School _____

11:30 to 11:50
  What:
  Materials:
  Where:
  TD or *IN*:
  WG, SG, 1 TO 1:

11:50 to 12:10
  What:
  Materials:
  Where:
  TD or *IN*:
  WG, SG, 1 TO 1:

12:10 to 12:30
  What:
  Materials:
  Where:
  TD or *IN*:
  WG, SG, 1 TO 1:

12:30 to 12:50
  What:
  Materials:
  Where:
  TD or *IN*:
  WG, SG, 1 TO 1:

12:50 to 1:10
  What:
  Materials:
  Where:
  TD or *IN*:
  WG, SG, 1 TO 1:

(continued)

Observation Sheet for Recording Literacy Activities in Whole-Day Programs (continued)

1:10 to 1:30
   What:
   Materials:
   Where:
   TD or *IN*:
   WG, SG, 1 TO 1:

1:30 to 1:50
   What:
   Materials:
   Where:
   TD or *IN*:
   WG, SG, 1 TO 1:

1:50 to 2:10
   What:
   Materials:
   Where:
   TD or *IN*:
   WG, SG, 1 TO 1:

2:10 to 2:30
   What:
   Materials:
   Where:
   TD or *IN*:
   WG, SG, 1 TO 1:

2:30 to 3:00
   What:
   Materials:
   Where:
   TD or *IN*:
   WG, SG, 1 TO 1:

Directions for Administering the Comprehension Test

Materials: Question-scoring sheet, storybook, and pencil

1. Read the story to the child. Tell the child that you will ask him or her questions about the story and will ask him or her to retell the story after you have read it.
2. After the story, read one question at a time to the child and write down the answer clearly in pencil.
3. Some questions have an open-ended part and then a multiple-choice part asking the same thing. Ask both parts even if the child answers the open-ended question correctly. They will receive more points for getting the open-ended question correct; however, we do not want you to have to make that decision as you are testing, so just ask both.
4. Do not supply answers or prompts but give children positive reinforcement whether they are right or wrong.

Comprehension Test: *Franklin in the Dark*: Structural Section

Child's Name _____ ID# _____

Teacher _____ ID# _____

1-Half-day, 2-Whole-day, 1-Male, 2-Female

Test ID# _____ 1-Pretest, 2-Posttest

Setting Questions

1. _____ What kind of animal is the most important in the story? What is his name? (main character, 2 points)
2. _____ Who are some of the other animals in the story? (other characters, 1 point each, maximum 4 points)
3. _____ Where does the story take place? (setting, 1 point)

Theme Questions

4. _____ What was the turtle's problem in the story? (theme, free recall 2 points, multiple choice, 1 point)
   _____ a. He was afraid to go in his shell because it was too small.
   _____ b. He was afraid to go in his shell because it was dark.

5. _____ List three things that Franklin did or that happened in the story.

6. _____ Of those you listed, which came first, second, and third? (1 point for proper order, no points for incorrect)

Resolution

7. _____ How did the turtle's problems get solved at the end of the story? (free recall, 2 points, multiple choice, 1 point)

_____ a. He finally went to sleep in his shell with a light on.

_____ b. His mother said he did not have to sleep in his shell.

Comprehension Test: *Franklin in the Dark*: Traditional Section

Literal Detail

8. _____ Name the animals Franklin met when he asked for help. (1 point each, maximum 3 points)

9. _____ How did Franklin bring his shell with him? (2 points)

Interpretive-Inference

10. _____ How do you think Franklin felt when he finally crawled into his shell at the end of the story? happy

sad _____

Why? (3 points with supported answer)

Critical: Compare and Contrast

11. What was it like for Franklin before he used a nightlight in his shell and what was it like for him after? (4 points; 2 for before, 2 for after)

Before the nightlight:

After the nightlight:

12. _____ Could this story have happened in real life?

_____ yes _____ no

13. _____ Why? (3 points with supported answer)

Comprehension Test: *Arthur's Eyes*: Structural Section

Child's Name _____ ID# _____

Teacher _____ ID# _____

1-Half-day, 2-Whole-day, 1-Male, 2-Female

Test ID# _____ 1-Pretest, 2-Posttest

Structural Section: Page 1

Setting Questions

1. _____ Who is the most important character (animal) in the story? What is his name? (main character, 2 points)
2. _____ Who are some of the other characters (animals) in the story? (1 point each, maximum 4 points)
3. _____ Where does the story take place? (setting 1 point)

Theme Questions

4. _____ What was Arthur's problem in the story? (theme, free recall 2 points)

   (Multiple choice, 1 point)

   ___ a. He did not want to wear his glasses

   ___ b. He would not do his schoolwork

Plot-Episode Questions

5. _____ List three things that Arthur did or that happened to him.
6. _____ Of those you listed which came first, second, and third? (1 for proper order, no points for incorrect)

Resolution Questions

7. _____ How did Arthur's problem get solved at the end of the story? (free recall, 2 points, multiple choice, 1 point)

   ___ a. He talked to the principal and decided to wear his glasses.

   ___ b. He broke his glasses and didn't have to wear them again.

Comprehension Test: *Arthur's Eyes*: Traditional Section

Literal Detail

8. _____ What are some of the things that happened to Arthur when he did not wear his glasses? (1 point per episode, 3 points maximum)

9. _____ How did Arthur try to lose his glasses? (2 points)

Interpretive-Inference

10. _____ How do you think Arthur felt when he decided to wear his glasses at the end of the story?

happy _____ sad _____

Why? (3 points with supported answer)

Critical: Compare and Contrast

11. _____ What was it like for Arthur before he had his glasses and what was it like for him after? (4 points; 2 for before, 2 for after)

Before getting glasses:

After getting glasses:

12. _____ Could this story have happened in real life?

Yes _____ No _____

13. _____ Why? (3 points with supported answer)

Administering Retelling Test

Materials to bring to testing:

Tape recorder, three tapes, storybook, and extra batteries

1. Identify on the tape the child's name, identification number, and teacher. Be sure the tape recorder is working properly.

2. Immediately following the comprehension tests, say to the child, "You just heard the story, _____, and I asked you some questions about it. Make believe I am your friend and I have never heard the story before and you try to tell it to me. We'll tape record it so you can hear some of the story. You can start with 'Once there was....'" You should also show the cover of the book, but do not let the child open it or look at the words or pictures.

3. Tape record the retelling. Do not give any cues or prompts. If the child has trouble starting, you can repeat, "Once there was..." or "Once upon a time...." If the child stops you may say, "Then what happened?" or "What comes next?" If the child seems to be done, you may say, "Can you think of anything else?" Use these exact words and use them only if the child needs help.

4. When the child is done, replay a little of the retelling. This will let you know it has recorded properly. In addition, the children enjoy it.

Story Retelling Analysis Oral and Written

Story Title _____

Place a one (1) next to each element if the child includes it in his or her presentation. Credit "gist" as well as obvious recall.

    I. _____ Setting (Maximum raw score 5 points)
       a. Begins story with an introduction _____
       b. Names main character _____
       c. Number of characters named _____
       d. Actual number of characters in story _____
       e. Score of other characters (c/d $\times$ 2) _____
       f. Includes statement of time or place _____

    II. _____ Theme (Maximum raw score, 2 quality answer, 1 for gist) Refers to main character's primary goal or problem to be solved.

    III. _____ Plot Episodes (Maximum 4 points)
       a. Number of episodes recalled _____
       b. Number of episodes in story _____
       c. Score for plot episodes (a/b $\times$ 4) _____

    IV. _____ Resolution (Maximum raw score, 2 points)
       a. Names problem solution or goal attained _____
       b. Ends the story _____

    V. _____ Sequence (2 points).
Retells story in structural order: setting, theme, plot episodes, and resolution (Score 2 for proper order, 1 for partial, 0 for no sequence evident)

    VI. _____ Total Retelling Score (Maximum 15 points)

Reenactment of Story

Child _____

Teacher _____

Sex: 1-M, 2-F

Kindergarten: 1-Whole day, 2-Half day

School _____

General Directionality

1-front to back   2-back to front

1-skipped pages   2-every page re-enacted

Pointing

at print: 1-yes   2-no

1-Frequently   2-moderately   3-infrequently

at pictures: 1-yes   2-no

1-Frequently,   2-moderately   3-infrequently

Eyes

on print: 1-yes   2-no

on pictures: 1-yes   2-no

cannot tell: 1-yes

other: 1-yes

_____

_____

_____

Story

Picture Governed, Story Not Formed. Child reads by labeling and relying on pictures. Little or no evidence of connected story-line.

1-yes   2-no

Picture Governed, Story Formed (Oral language-like). Child focused on pictures. Uses oral language style while commenting on pictures. May tell interesting story but language is unlike that of a book.

1-yes   2-no

Picture Governed, Story Formed (Oral language and Written language-mixed)

Child alternates among oral language style and reading intonation and working that sounds like written language. At times reading may sound very much like written language of a book.

1-yes   2-no

Picture Governed, Story Formed (Written language-like). Reading is very much like written language of a text. Some attempts may be made at decoding recognizable words.

1-yes   2-no

Print Governed. Child reads in a conventional manner.

1-yes   2-no

Teacher Rating Scale

Children's Reading Ability and Interest in Reading

Using the scale 1 (very low), 2 (low), 3 (moderate), 4 (high), and 5 (very high), rate each child on both reading ability and interest in reading. Rate all the children on reading ability before rating them on interest.

When rating children's ability, consider the following guidelines:

1 (very low)—more than 1 year below grade level

2 (low)—1 year below grade level

3 (moderate)—on grade level

4 (high)—1 year above grade level

5 (very high)—more than 1 year above grade level

When rating children's interest in reading and literature, consider the following questions:

During free-choice time, does the child choose to look at books?

When the child is done with other work does he or she choose to read or look at books?

Does the child take out books from the school or classroom library?

Does the child ever share books with others?

Teacher _____

Child's Name _____

Reading ability: 1, 2, 3, 4, 5

Reading interest: 1, 2, 3, 4, 5

Kindergarten Inventory of Concepts About Print and Emergent Reading Checklist

Child _____

Teacher _____

Sex: 1-M, 2-F

1-pretest, 2-posttest

Kindergarten: 1-Whole day, 2-Half day

School _____

Put a familiar book on the table. Ask the child to pick it up and show you the following items. For example, "Show me the front cover. Now show me the back cover."

For all questions circle 1 for right, 2 for wrong.

Front cover: 1   2

Back cover: 1   2

Title or name of story: 1   2

Name of the author: 1   2

Open to a page with some print and ask child to show you each of the following:

Top of page: 1   2

Bottom of page: 1   2

Word: 1   2

Letter: 1   2

Capital letter: 1   2

Lower-case or smaller letter: 1   2

Point to where it tells the reader to say.

Points to print: 1   2

Show me where the reader starts to read the story.

Turns to the front of book: 1   2

Show me where the reader stops reading at the end of the story.

Turns to back of book: 1   2

Have a word on a 3 × 5 card that is on a page of the book. Turn to the page of the book.

Show me this word on the page.

Shows the word: 1   2

Adapted from Marie Clay (1985) *The early detection of reading difficulties* (3rd Edition). Portsmouth NH: Heinemann.

Interview Questions

1. Do you get tired in school? 1-yes   2-no
2. If you get tired, when do you get tired?
   1-early in the morning   2-after lunch
   3-when it's time to go home.
Open-ended answer below:
3. Do you think school is too long? 1-yes   2-no
4. If you think it is too long why?
   1-I get tired   2-I get bored   3-It isn't fun
Open-ended answer below:
5. Would you like to be at school for a longer time every day?
   1-yes   2-no
6. Why would you like school to be longer?
   1-I have nothing to do at home   2-we do good things
Open-ended answer here:

Teacher Interview

Teacher's Name _____

School _____

Type of Kindergarten: Circle one: Half day, Whole day

1. How long have you been teaching?
2. When did you teach kindergarten last?
3. What grade did you teach (if it is not kindergarten) most recently and for how long?
4. For how many years have you taught kindergarten?
5. What do you like about teaching half-day kindergarten?
6. What don't you like about a half-day kindergarten program?
7. In your half-day program now, or when you used to teach half day, describe how much time in each school day you spend on literacy activities such as reading and writing.
8. Describe the nature of these literacy activities: whole-class lessons, activity worksheets, group work, and skill development.
9. What do you think you would like or do like about a whole-day kindergarten program?
10. What do you think you would not like or don't like about a whole-day kindergarten program?

11. In your whole-day kindergarten, or if you were in a whole-day kindergarten, describe how much time is or would be spent on literacy activities in each school day.
12. Describe the nature of the activities in literacy in a whole-day kindergarten (Whole class, worksheets, group work, skill development, or integrated in content areas.)
13. Do you believe students will score better on achievement tests related to literacy based on the fact that they are in a whole-day program or a half-day program?
14. If you had your choice, would you rather teach in a whole-day kindergarten program or in a half-day? Regardless of your choice, give reasons for your answer.
15. Do you feel it is better for children to attend whole-day or half-day kindergarten? Support your answer.
16. What are your goals for the kindergarten program?
17. What are the district's goals for the kindergarten program?
18. Are your goals the same?
19. Describe how you plan your school day:
    What content areas do you include?
    How much time for each area?
    What types of organizational plans, whole-group, small-group, one-to-one meetings?
20. What can you do differently in a whole-day kindergarten and half-day kindergarten as far as literacy instruction is concerned?

Samples of Categorized Anecdotal Observations Collected for the Study

Category: Comprehension Development While Storybook Reading

Description: The book *Gilberto and the Wind* was being reviewed. A chart with two columns stating whether the wind was "nice" or "not nice" was used to talk about certain parts of the story.

Teacher: Let's read the name of the story we read yesterday. Now look this way and follow my finger. Ready.

Students: Gil-berto and the wind.

Teacher: In this book the author and the illustrator are the same person. And that person is Marie Hall Ets. Let's zip through the pages and see if you can tell me about different parts of the story. We already read it, so you know the story. (The teacher goes through the story page by page to review and points to the pictures as she does. She stops to talk about different parts of the story along the way.)

G1: The wind blow the balloon in tree.

Teacher: Right! The wind blew the balloon in the tree. Was the wind nice to Gilberto or not nice?

Students: Not nice!

Teacher: Right. So Jane told us about when the wind was not being nice to Gilberto. Let's read it. (She points to the chart.)

Students: Balloon!

Teacher: Balloon! Right. That was the last part with the balloon. What's the first letter you hear in *ba-ba-balloon*? Everybody.

Students: *B*!

Teacher: What's the last letter you hear in *balloon*? *Balloonnnn.* Everybody.

Students: *N*!

Teacher: Raise your hands if you could tell me what happened with the wash on the line?

B1: The wind blew the clothes.

Teacher: The wind was blowing the clothes. When the wind blew it very, very hard what happened to the clothes?

B1: It fell.

Teacher: What do you think would happen when the mommy or the other big people in the house—when they saw the clothes on the ground? Can you predict how they might feel?

B1: Saaad.

Teacher: Yes, sad. They might even be angry or annoyed. OK, so was the wind being nice with the clothes or not nice?

Students: Not nice!

Teacher: OK. Let's read. The wind was...

Students: Not nice with wash on the line!

Teacher: OK, the next thing Gilberto had in his hand was? Everybody.

Students: Umbrella!

Teacher: OK, and everyone says the word again.

Students: *Ummmbrella.*

Teacher: *Umbrella*! Who can tell me what happened? What happened to that umbrella?

G2: Umm. It went inside out.

Teacher: It went inside out. Who made it go inside out?

Students: The wind.

Teacher: The wind. How do you think the wind made it go inside out? Raise your hands.

G2: Blowing.

Teacher: And did it blow just a little? How do you think it blew? Just a little bit or a lot? Can you describe how the wind blew that umbrella inside out?

B1: It blew hard.

Teacher: Yes. It blew very, very, very hard. So over here was the wind being nice or not nice?

Students: Not nice!

Teacher: Now we have the umbrella in the not nice column. Who could tell me what this part is about? What happened?

B2: Gilberto when he was swingin' on the gate when the wind, the wind blow and let it go inside out.

Teacher: OK, the wind was making the gate go where? In and out where it was opening and closing the gate. It was blowing the gate open and close. What did Gilberto want to do?

Students: Swing.

Teacher: He wanted to swing and he wanted to take a ride on the gate. OK. Did the wind get to blow Gilberto on the gate?

Students: Nooo.

Teacher: The wind wouldn't blow strong enough and Gilberto was too heavy. So was the wind being nice or not nice with the gate?

Students: Not nice.

Teacher: Not nice. Sure enough. What number is next to the word *gate*.

B3: Six.

Teacher: This is number six, you're right.

Teacher: Right. Now, this is the part with the kites that the big boys were flying. Who remembers about the kites and the big boys? Who could tell me about that part of the story? What happened to the kite with the big boys? The wind was what?

Students: Nice!

Teacher: With the big—let's read it together.

Students: Big boys kite.

Teacher: But what about Gilberto's kite? Was the wind nice or not nice to Gilberto's kite?

Students: Not nice!

Teacher: Yes! Read with me.

Students: The wind was not nice with Gilberto's kite.

Teacher: So poor Gilberto. The wind was not nice with Gilberto's kite. Oh. Remember this part? OK. Who can tell me about this part? OK. Where was Gilberto? Is he in the tree or under the tree?

Some Students: Under!

Teacher: Under the tree. He didn't have to climb in the tree. All he had to do was stand under the tree and the wind— what? Everybody.

Students: Shook apples down from tree.

Teacher: So. Over here it says apples. Good. And was the wind being nice or not nice? Nice. OK, here let's skip to the end. Gilberto wanted to take a rest. Did the wind blow big and strong and make a lot of howling noises to keep him up?

Students: Noooo!

Teacher: No. The wind was being nice—or not nice?

Students: Nice.

Teacher: He was being nice when Gilberto wanted to sleep. OK. How many things was the wind being nice to...over here. All together.

Students: One, two, three, four, five, six.

Teacher: How many things did we find when the wind was be-ing—what?

Students: Not nice! One, two, three, four, five, six, seven.

Teacher: Which one is bigger? Six or seven?

Students: Seven.

Teacher: Seven. Seven is more than six. OK. This is what we did yesterday. We did a good job with that.

Category: Oral Language and Integration of Literacy Into Content Areas

Description: The teacher stood in front of the class. The book *Stone Soup* was on the ledge of the easel. The children were seated at their tables. The theme was Good Nutrition and they had read the book *Stone Soup* and were going to prepare stone soup.

Teacher: We are going to go to Food Town today to buy what we need to make our Stone Soup. Where would we find the stone?

Students: On the ground!

Teacher: Whatever stone we find today I am going to bring it home. I am going to scrub it. I am going to scrub it with soap and water.

Students: No!

Teacher: Put it in a pot, boil it for an hour, and all the bacteria will be out of it and all germs will be gone. I will make sure all the soap is off it, so all the germs are off it and we have to put it in our soup because that is the number one ingredient.

The teacher shows the students a shopping list that she has written out. The list is hung on the easel with the words *crackers*, *bread*, *corn*, *beans*, *bowls*, and *spoons*.

(The teacher points to the list.)

Teacher: What is one of the ingredients?

B1: Butter.

Teacher: We can use some butter.

Teacher: What else do we have to get?

B2: I know…

(Students raise their hands.)

Teacher: What is this?

Students: Crackers!

Teacher: Yes.

Teacher: What else do we have to get?

Teacher: We are also going to have beef cubes and in order to make it a little tastier we have to add two spices.

(Student calls out.)

B3:   Salt and pepper.

G3:   Butter.

Teacher: And lastly, this is a tough one.

(Students raise their hands.)

B4:   Barley.

Teacher: That was good.

Teacher: We decided that we do not want barley; instead of barley we would buy corn.

Teacher: Now what else did we say we wanted? We are going to get the kind of corn in a can. What other vegetable are we going to get that is green?

Students: Green beans.

Teacher: What do we need to put our soup in? (She looks to the chart.)

B4:   Bowls.

Students: Spoons.

(The teacher points to the words as she says them.)

Teacher: She also used tomatoes, but I'm not going to put tomatoes in it, because a lot of you don't like tomatoes. Now another thing we said we wanted were noodles, before we go to the store we have to decide what kind of noodles we want. We could all decide.

B5:   I don't like noodles.

Teacher: Well then you don't have to eat them. We are going to have a vote.

(The teacher wrote down three kinds of noodles on the chart paper; alphabet, curly, and shells.)

Teacher: How many people want alphabet noodles?

(Students raise their hands to vote and the teacher counts the students out loud. She counts 12 and writes it on the chart paper.)

Teacher: You can only vote once, if you voted you can't vote again. Curly ones?

(The students raise their hands. She counts aloud five students and writes it down.)

Teacher: Who wants the shell kind?

(One person raises her hand. The teacher writes this down.)

Teacher: Well it looks like the ABC noodles. Before we go I am going to read you a story.

During the lesson the teacher continued to make reference to the shopping list she had created by pointing to the words.

Category: Writing Activities

Description: After buying the ingredients to make stone soup at the supermarket, the teacher is in front of the class while the students are seated at their tables. The items they purchased are on the table and the shopping list is on the easel for everyone to see. The teacher gives the students their journals and a pencil.

Teacher: Everyone open to the next clean page in your journal and draw a picture and write a sentence about our shopping day. Miss A, Mrs. T, and I will go around and you tell us what you wrote. What did you like about the morning? Let's draw something about shopping.

(The teachers go around the room and write what the students dictate if they can't write it themselves. The teacher is circulating around the room. Some of the students are finished and they begin to get up.)

Teacher's aide: No, no, finish your picture. Have you finished B2?

B2: Yeah.

Teacher's aide: Write something about it in your own words.

(The teacher is speaking to a student.)

Teacher: You drew a picture. Good!

B3: I'm done.

Teacher: That's beautiful G1. Are you ready, G2?

(B4 comes up to teacher who is working with G3 and reads to her what was written in his journal.)

B4: I went to the store.

Teacher: That's very good.

G2: I'm writing the date.

Teacher: Great.

(As the students finish writing, their journals are collected.)

During the journal writing time the students talked among themselves. The teacher prompted the students to tell her what they had written or drawn.

Category: Knowledge About Print

Description: The teacher stood in front of the group sitting on the rug in the literacy corner. The teacher positioned herself by the large paper pad on the easel to write sentences about the day.

Teacher: Who can gave us a sentence telling us about today? G1? Wait. We didn't do the calendar, did we? (Class: Noooo.) OK. How about if you stay here and B1, it's your turn; you come up with me. OK, come on up...Go ahead.

B1: (Uses the pointer and hesitates between words) Today is sunny and cold.

Teacher: OK. Do you want to leave that up? (B1 shakes his head) Great job. Let's go over the days of the week. *Sunday...Saturday*. (points to each word, students join in on *Monday*; the teacher goes at a fast pace) Today is *Thhhursday*. (teacher starts word and waits for the students to join in) OK. We're in the month of February and B1 is going to count for us. Go ahead.

B1: One, Two...Eight, Nine.

Teacher: That's it! Today is February 9, Thhuursday, February 9th. Let's give B1 a nice hand! (scattered claps as she walks back to the easel) OK. G1 is going to give me a sentence about *today*. *T...o...d...a...y* What word? (some answer after she writes it on the paper) What word is this? (all answer) *Today*...G1?"

G1: Today is...

Teacher: Is, i...s...What day of the week is it G1? Monday, Tuesday, Wednesday...(students join in for the chant).

G1: Thursday.

Teacher: Thursday, great! Capital *T*, because it's the name of a day, *h...u...r...s...d...a...y*. What month? G1? (no reply) What month is it B2?

B2: February.

Teacher: Capital *F*, because it's the name of a month, *e...b...r...u...a...r...y*. What number is it G1? Take a look at the calendar. What number?

G1: (goes to the board) Nine.

Teacher: February 9, comma. What year G1? (student closes eyes to think) Look and find the year. There you go. Great, G1. (students have been joining in as the teacher writes things on the paper) OK. Who would like to tell us anything about the weather? And I'm going to start off the sentence a little bit differently by saying, The, the beginning of the sentence so capital *T*; *The weather*, *w...e...a...t...h...e...r..*, *the weather is*...Who could complete the sentence? B3?...What is the weather like outside?

B3: It's cold and sunny. (random students call out with him)

B1: (called out, saying something about looking for *k*s)

Teacher: Ohhh. Are we looking for *K*s?

Students: Yessss.

Teacher: What letter are we working on? (Students: *k*sssss. We got to look for *K*ss.) Oh I see. We'll look later. All right, can we add to that? Give us another sentence telling us about today. Anything special about today?

B1:	Today, a, a, is, um...(Teacher: Thursday) Today...I'm going to have a party at my house.
Teacher:	You're having a party today? OK. What kind of a party?
B2:	I think, I think, I think it's my sister's party (shrugs shoulders).
Teacher:	OK. (Students question what kind of a party.) Where are you having the party?
B3:	At my house.
Teacher:	(Writes: at his house; G1 helps with saying the sentence; students comment on how they're going to have a birthday party too.) What else is special about yesterday, today, tomorrow?
G2:	We're going to read a book?
Teacher:	We do that every day. What's different about yesterday, today, tomorrow? Listen to the word yesterday. Yesterday was Wednesday, tomorrow is Friday.
G3:	Yesterday we had music.
Teacher:	Yes. Yesterday we had music. OK. (starts writing the sentence) Capital *Y*, beginning of a sentence, *Yesterday we had music.*
B2:	I know that starts with a *Y*: *yyyyyy.*
Teacher:	OK. What time are we going home today? What time did we go home yesterday? What time are we going home tomorrow? Who could give me a sentence telling me about that? (students chatter among themselves) Who could give me a sentence telling me about that? B4?
B4:	One o'clock.
Teacher:	*We*, capital *W*, because it's the beginning of a sentence, *We will be going*, *g...o...i...n...g*. Going where? (writes as the students call out) home at...at what time? (students call out 1:00 and 1:30) One o'clock, not 1:30. And how do we write 1:00? One, dot, dot, zero, zero (followed writing at the speed the children called out.) Did we learn that? (Students: Yesss.) What clock would read like that? (Students: Digital.) A digital clock. Very good.

Category: Free-Choice Center Time

Description: During free-choice center time, children chose to play with the letters of the alphabet on a flannel board. All other focus children are at various centers around the room. The teacher is circling the room helping students when necessary.

G1:   We're writing our ABCs.

Teacher: That's right. What are you doing?

G2:   Putting up the letters with G1.

Teacher: Very good. Let's talk about them as we do them.

G3:   Look, I made a *d*.

Teacher: What is that?

G3:   Oh, a *q*.

G1:   It's a *q*.

Teacher: What letter is that?

G3:   *b*.

Teacher: Say the alphabet for me, please.

G3 & G1: (They continue to put up the letters in proper order. When they get stuck, they recite the alphabet for help.)

G3:   How do you spell your name?

Teacher: What do you think it starts with? (Says G2's name)

G3:   *D*?

Teacher: Yes. Very good. Use a capital letter, now a lower case comes next because you just started the name with a capital letter.

References

Adams, A. & Bruno, R. (1993). *School enrollment social and economic characteristics of students.* Washington, DC: U.S. Department of Commerce.

Adams, M.J. (1990). *Beginning to read: Thinking and learning about print.* Urbana, IL: University of Illinois Center for the Study of Reading.

Alvermann, D.E., O'Brien, D.G., & Dillon, D.R. (1990). What teachers do when they say they're having discussions of content area reading assignments: A qualitative analysis. *Reading Research Quarterly, 25,* 296–322.

Bandura, A. (1989). *Social foundations of thought and action: A social cognitive theory.* Englewood Cliffs, NJ: Prentice Hall.

Barker, L.L. (1963). *The stream of behavior: Explorations of its structure and content.* New York: Appleton-Century-Crofts.

Barnard, H. (Ed.). (1981). *Papers on Froebel's kindergarten, with suggestions on principles and methods of child culture in different countries.* Hartford, CT: Office of Barnard's American Journal of Education. (Republished from the *American Journal of Education*)

Biklen, S.K., & Bogdan, R. (1982). *Qualitative research for education: An introduction to theory and methods.* Boston, MA: Allyn & Bacon.

Bloom, B. (1972). *Language development: Form and function in emerging grammars.* Cambridge, MA: Massachusetts Institute of Technology Press.

Bredekamp, S. & Copple, C. (Eds.). (1997). *Developmentally appropriate practice in early childhood programs* (Revised ed.). Washington, DC: National Association for the Education of Young Children.

Brown, R. (1973). *A first language: The early stages.* Cambridge, MA: Harvard University Press.

Brown, R., & Bellugi, U. (1964). Three processes in the child's acquisition of syntax. *Harvard Educational Review, 34,* 133–151.

Bruner, J. (1975). The ontogenesis of speech acts. *Journal of Child Language, 3,* 1–19.

Bruno, R., & Adams, A. (1993). *School enrollment—social and economic characteristics of students: October 1993* (Bureau of the Census's Current

Population Reports, Population Characteristics P20–479). Washington, DC: U.S. Bureau of the Census.

Bryant, D., & Clifford, R. (1992). 150 years of kindergarten: How far have we come? *Early Childhood Research Quarterly, 7*, 147–154.

Calkins, L.M. (1983). *Lessons from a child: On the teaching and learning of writing.* Portsmouth, NH: Heinemann.

Clark, M.M. (1976). *Young fluent readers.* London: Heinemann.

Clay, M.M. (1966). *Emergent reading behavior.* Unpublished doctoral dissertation, University of Auckland, New Zealand.

Clay, M.M. (1985). *Early detection of reading difficulties* (3rd ed.). Portsmouth, NH: Heinemann.

Cohen, D. (1968). The effects of literature on vocabulary and reading achievement. *Elementary English, 45*, 209–213, 217.

Corsaro, W. (1985). *Friendship and peer culture in the early years.* Norwood, NJ: Ablex.

Cryan, J., Sheehan, R., Wiechel, J., & Bandy-Hedden, I. (1992). Success outcomes of full-day kindergarten: More positive behavior and increased achievement in the years after. *Early Childhood Research Quarterly, 7*, 187–203.

Csikszentimihalyi, M. (1991). Literacy and intrinsic motivation. In S.R. Graubard (Ed.), *Literacy: An overview by fourteen experts.* New York: Farrar, Straus & Giroux.

Dewey, J. (1966). *Democracy and education.* New York: Free Press.

Durkin, D. (1966). *Children who read early.* New York: Teachers College Press.

Erickson, H.L. (1995). *Stirring the head, heart, and soul.* Thousand Oaks, CA: Corwin Press.

Feitelson, D., Kita, B., & Goldstein, Z. (1986). Effects of listening to series stories on first graders' comprehension and use of language. *Research in the Teaching of English, 20*, 339–356.

Fetterman, D.M. (1984). *Ethnography in educational evaluation.* Beverly Hills, CA: Sage Publications.

Field, T. (1980). Preschool play: Effects of teacher/child ratios and organization of classroom space. *Child Study Journal, 10*, 191–205.

Flesch, R. (1955). *Why Johnny Can't Read.* New York: Harper & Row.

Forman, E., & Cazden, C. (1985). Exploring Vygotskian perspectives in education: The cognitive value of peer interaction. In J. Wertsch (Ed.), *Culture, communication, and cognition: Vygotskian perspectives.* Cambridge, England: Cambridge University Press.

Froebel, F. (1974). *The education of man.* Clifton, NJ: Augustus, Kelly.

Fromberg, D. (1986). *The full-day kindergarten.* New York: Teachers College Press.

Fromberg, D.P. (1992). Implementing the full-day kindergarten. *Principal*, *71*, 26–28.

Gilstrap, R. (1970). The case for full-time kindergarten. *School Administrator*, *27*, 15–21.

Goodman, Y. (1984). The development of initial literacy. In H. Goelman, A. Oberg, & F. Smith (Eds.), *Awakening to literacy* (pp. 102–109). Portsmouth, NH: Heinemann.

Gorton, H.B., & Robinson, R.L. (1968). For better results—A full-day kindergarten. *Education*, *89*, 217–221.

Green, J.L., & Wallat, C. (Eds.). (1981). *Ethnography and language in educational settings*. Norwood, NJ: Ablex.

Harrison-McEachern, R. (1989, December). *Half-day kindergarten versus all-day kindergarten and its effects on first grade reading achievement*. Master's thesis, Kean College of New Jersey, Union.

Hatcher, B., & Schmidt, V. (1990). Half-day vs. full-day kindergarten programs. *Childhood Education*, *57*, 14–17.

Herman, B. (1984). *The case for the all-day kindergarten*. Bloomington, IN: Phi Delta Kappa.

Hoffman, S.J. (1982). *Preschool reading related behaviors: A parent diary*. Unpublished doctoral dissertation, University of Pennsylvania, Philadelphia.

Holdaway, D. (1979). *The foundations of literacy*. Sydney, Australia: Ashton Scholastic.

Holdaway, D. (1986). The structure of natural learning as a basis for literacy instruction. In M. Sampson (Ed.), *The pursuit of literacy: Early reading and writing*. Dubuque, IA: Kendall/Hunt.

Holmes, C.T., & McConnell, B.M. (1990, April). *Full-day versus half-day kindergarten: An experimental study*. Paper presented at the annual meeting of the American Educational Research Association, Boston, MA.

Housden, T., & Kam, R. (1992). *Full-day kindergarten: A summary of the research*. Carmichael, CA: San Juan Unified School District. (ERIC Document Reproduction Service No. ED 345 868)

Humphrey, J.W. (1980). *A study of the effectiveness of full-day kindergarten*. (ERIC Document Reproduction Service No. ED 190 224)

Humphrey, J.W. (1983). A comparison of full-day and half-day kindergartens. *ERS Spectrum*, *1*, 11–16.

Humphrey, J.W. (1990). *Feasibility study concerning mandatory half-day kindergarten and mandatory and voluntary full-day kindergarten*. Prepared for the Indiana Department of Education. (ERIC Document Reproduction Service No. ED 327 268)

International Reading Association. (1990). *Literacy development and prefirst grade*. Newark, DE: Author.

Johnson, D.W., & Johnson, R.T. (1987). *Learning together and alone* (2nd ed.). Englewood Cliffs, NJ: Prentice Hall.

Juel, C., Griffith, P.L., & Gough, P.B. (1986). Acquisition of literacy: A longitudinal study of children in first and second grade. *Journal of Educational Psychology, 78,* 243–255.

Karweit, N. (1992). The kindergarten experience. *Educational Leadership, 49,* 82–86.

Lennenberg, E. (1967). *Biological foundations of language.* New York: Wiley.

Lincoln, Y., & Guba, E. (1985). *Naturalistic inquiry.* Beverly Hills, CA: Sage.

Maehr, M.L. (1976). Continuing motivation: An analysis of a seldom considered educational outcome. *Review of Educational Research, 46,* 443–462.

Mandler, J., & Johnson, N. (1977). Remembrance of things parsed: Story structure and recall. *Cognitive Psychology, 9,* 111–151.

Mason, J. (1984). Early reading from a developmental perspective. In P.D. Pearson, M. Kamil, P. Mosenthal, & R. Barr (Eds.), *Handbook of reading research: Volume 1.* New York: Longman.

Mason, J., & Au, K. (1990). *Reading instruction for today* (2nd ed.). Reading, MA: Addison-Wesley.

McCombs, B.L. (1991). Unraveling motivation: New perspectives from research and practice. *The Journal of Experimental Education, 60,* 3–88.

McNeil, D. (1970). *The acquisition of language: The study of developmental psycholinguistics.* New York: Harper & Row.

Menyuk, P. (1977). *Language and maturation.* Cambridge, MA: Massachusetts Institute of Technology Press.

Miles, M.B., & Huberman, A.M. (1984). Drawing valid meaning from qualitative data: Towards a shared craft. *Educational Researcher, 13*(4), 20–30.

Monson, D., & Sebesta, S. (1991). Reading preferences. In J. Flood, J. Jensen, D. Lapp, & J. Squire (Eds.), *Handbook of research on teaching the English language arts* (pp. 664–673). New York: Macmillan.

Montessori, M. (1965). *Spontaneous activity in education.* New York: Schocken Books.

Moore, G. (1986). Effects of the spatial definition of behavior settings on children's behavior: A quasi-experimental field study. *Journal of Environmental Psychology, 6,* 205–231.

Morrow, L.M. (1983). Home and school correlates of early interest in literature. *Journal of Educational Research, 76,* 121–130.

Morrow, L.M. (1984). Reading stories to young children: Effects of story structure and traditional questioning strategies on comprehension. *Journal of Reading Behavior, 16,* 273–288.

Morrow, L.M. (1985). Retelling stories: A strategy for improving children's comprehension, concept of story structure and oral language complexity. *The Elementary School Journal, 85,* 647–661.

Morrow, L.M. (1987). Promoting voluntary reading: The effects of an inner city program in summer day care centers. *The Reading Teacher, 41,* 266–274.

Morrow, L.M. (1988). Young children's responses to one-to-one story readings in school settings. *Reading Research Quarterly, 23,* 89–107.

Morrow, L.M. (1992). The impact of a literature-based program on literacy achievement, use of literature, and attitudes of children from minority backgrounds. *Reading Research Quarterly, 27,* 250–275.

Morrow, L.M. (1993). *Literacy development in the early years: Helping children read and write* (2nd ed.). Needham Heights, MA: Allyn & Bacon.

Morrow, L.M. (1996). *Motivating reading and writing in diverse classrooms: Social and physical contexts in a literature-based program* (NCTE Research Report No. 28). Urbana, IL: National Council of Teachers of English.

Morrow, L.M. (1997a). *Literacy development in the early years: Helping children read and write* (3rd ed.). Needham Heights, MA: Allyn & Bacon.

Morrow, L.M. (1997b). *The Literacy Center: Contexts for reading and writing.* York, ME: Stenhouse Publishers

Morrow, L.M., O'Connor, E.M., & Smith, J. (1990). Effects of a storyreading program on the literacy development of at-risk kindergarten children. *Journal of Reading Behavior, 20*(2), 104–141.

Morrow, L.M., & Rand, M. (1991). Promoting literacy during play by designing early childhood classroom environments. *The Reading Teacher, 44,* 396–402.

Morrow, L.M., & Smith, J.K. (1990). The effects of group settings on interactive storybook reading. *Reading Research Quarterly, 25,* 213–231.

Morrow, L.M., & Weinstein, C.S. (1986). Encouraging voluntary reading: The impact of a literature program on children's use of library centers. *Reading Research Quarterly, 21,* 330–346.

Naron, N.K. (1981). The need for full-day kindergarten. *Educational Leadership, 38,* 306–309.

Neiman, R.H., & Gastright, J.F. (1981). The long-term effects of Title 1 preschool and all-day kindergarten. *Phi Delta Kappan, 63,* 184–185.

Neuman, S., & Roskos, K. (1992). Literacy objects as cultural tools: Effects on children's literacy behaviors in play. *Reading Research Quarterly, 27,* 202–225.

Neuman, S.B., & Roskos, K. (1993). Access to print for children of poverty: Differential effects of parent mediation and literacy-enriched play settings on environmental and functional print tasks for African-American children reared in poverty. *American Educational Research Journal, 32,* 801–828.

Ninio, A. (1980). Picture book reading in mother-infant dyads belonging to two subgroups in Israel. *Child Development, 51,* 587–590.

Oelerich, M. (1979). *Kindergarten: All-day everyday?* Mankato, MN: Mankato State University. (ERIC Document Reproduction Service No. ED 179 282)

Ogle, D.M. (1986). K-W-L: A teaching model that develops active reading of expository text. *The Reading Teacher, 39*, 564–570.

Oldfather, P. (1993). What students say about motivating experiences in a whole language classroom. *The Reading Teacher, 46*, 672–681.

Peck, J., McCaig, G., & Sapp, M. (1988). *Kindergarten policies: What is best for children?* Washington, DC: National Association for the Education of Young Children.

Pellegrini, A., & Galda, L. (1982). The effects of thematic fantasy play training on the development of children's story comprehension. *American Educational Research Journal, 19*, 443–452.

Peskin, M. (1988). *Are social and economic changes in family patterns dictating the frequency and curriculum of all-day kindergarten?* Seton Hall, NJ: Seton Hall University College of Education. (ERIC Document Reproduction Service No. 293 647)

Piaget, J. (1959). *The language and thought of the child* (3rd ed.). London: Routledge & Kegan Paul.

Piaget, J., & Inhelder, B. (1969). *The psychology of the child.* New York: Basic Books.

Puleo, V. (1988). A review and critique of research on full-day kindergarten. *The Elementary School Journal, 88*, 427–439.

Rand, M.K. (1994). Using thematic instruction to organize an integrated language arts classroom. In L.M. Morrow, J.K. Smith, & L.C. Wilkinson (Eds.), *Integrated Language Arts: Controversy to consensus.* Boston, MA: Allyn & Bacon.

Ross, E.D. (1976). *The kindergarten crusade: The establishment of preschool education in the United States.* Athens, OH: Ohio University Press.

Rothenberg, D. (1995). *Full-day kindergarten programs. ERIC Digest* (ERIC Document Reproduction Service No. ED 383 410)

Rusk, R., & Scotland, J. (1979). *Doctrines of the great educators.* New York: St. Martin's Press.

Schickedanz, J. (1986). *More than ABC's: The early stages of reading and writing.* Washington, DC: National Association for the Education of Young Children.

Schickedanz, J.A. (1993). Designing the early childhood classroom environment to facilitate literacy development. In B. Spodek & O.N. Saracho (Eds.), *Language and literacy in early childhood education: Yearbook in early childhood education* (Vol. 4). New York: Teachers College Press.

Skinner, E., & Belmont, M. (1993). Motivation in the classroom: Reciprocal effect of teacher behavior and student engagement across the school year. *Journal of Educational Psychology, 85*, 571–581.

Smith, F. (1971). *Understanding reading*. New York: Holt, Rinehart, & Winston.

Smith, F. (1983). A metaphor for literacy: Creating words or shunting information? In F. Smith (Ed.), *Essays into literacy*. Portsmouth, NH: Heinemann.

Strickland, D.S. (1990). Emergent literacy: How young children learn to read. *Educational Leadership, 47*, 18–23.

Strickland, D.S. (1995). Reinventing our literacy programs: Books, basics, balance. *The Reading Teacher, 48*, 294–302.

Strickland, D.S, & Morrow, L.M. (1989). *Emerging literacy: Young children learn to read and write*. Newark, DE: International Reading Association.

Sulzby, E. (1985). Children's emergent reading of favorite storybooks. *Reading Research Quarterly, 20*, 458–481.

Sulzby, E. (1986). Kindergartners as writers and readers. In M. Farr (Ed.), *Advances in writing research: Children's early writing* (Vol. 1, pp. 127–200). Norwood, NJ: Ablex.

Teale, W. (1978). Positive environments for learning to read: What studies of early readers tell us. *Language Arts, 55*, 922–932.

Teale, W. (1982). Toward a theory of how children learn to read and write naturally. *Language Arts, 59*, 555–570.

Teale, W. (1986). The beginning of reading and writing: Written language development during the preschool and kindergarten years. In M. Sampson (Ed.), *The pursuit of literacy: Early reading and writing*. Dubuque, IA: Kendall/Hunt.

Teale, W., & Sulzby, E. (1986). Emergent literacy as a perspective for looking at how children become writers and readers. In W.H. Teale & E. Sulzby (Eds.), *Emergent literacy: Writing and reading* (pp. vii–xxv). Norwood, NJ: Ablex.

Terens, S. (1984). *Second year full-day kindergarten program evaluation, Lawrence Public Schools, No. 4 school*. Paper presented to the American Educational Research Association, New Orleans, LA. (ERIC Document Reproduction Service No. ED 251 177)

Thorndyke, P. (1977). Cognitive structures in comprehension and memory of narrative discourse. *Cognitive Psychology, 9*, 77–110.

Towers, J.M. (1991). Attitudes toward the all-day everyday kindergarten. *Children Today, 29*(1), 25–28.

Turner, J.C. (1995). The influence of classroom contexts on young children's motivation for literacy. *Reading Research Quarterly, 30*, 410–441.

U.S. Department of Commerce. (1995). Statistical abstract of the United States 1995. In *The national data book* (p. 406). Washington, DC: Author.

U.S. Department of Education National Center for Education Statistics. (1996). *Ages for compulsory school attendance, special education services for students, state policies for kindergarten programs, and year-round schools by state, 1995–1996*. Washington, DC: Author.

Vygotsky, L.S. (1978). *Mind in society: The development of higher psychological processes*. (M. Cole, V. John-Steiner, S. Scribner, & E. Souberman, Eds. and Trans.). Cambridge, MA: Harvard University Press. (Original work published 1934)

Vygotsky, L.S. (1981). The genesis of higher mental functions. In J.J. Wertsch (Ed.), *The concept of activity*. White Plains, NY: M.E. Sharpe.

Walsh, D. (1989). Changes in kindergarten: Why here? Why now? *Early Childhood Research Quarterly, 4*, 377–391.

Washington, T., Lee, K., Thomson, P., Moomgy, C. & Gable, C. (1993). *New Brunswick public school early childhood curriculum manual for pre-k and kindergarten*. New Brunswick, NJ: New Brunswick Public Schools.

Webster, N.K. (1984). The 5's and 6's go to school, revisited. *Childhood Education, 60*, 325–330.

Wittrock, M.C. (1986). Students' thought processes. In M.C. Wittrock (Ed.), *Handbook of research on teaching* (pp. 297–314). New York: Macmillan.

Children's Literature References

Bemelmans, L. (1939). *Madeline*. New York: Viking.

Bourgeois, P. (1986). *Franklin in the dark*. New York: Scholastic.

Brown, M. (1976). *One, two, three: An animal counting book*. Boston, MA: Little, Brown.

Brown, M. (1979). *Arthur's eyes*. Boston, MA: Little, Brown.

Carle, E. (1968). *1, 2, 3 to the zoo*. New York: William Collins.

dePaola, T. (1973). *Charlie needs a clock*. Englewood Cliffs, NJ: Prentice Hall.

Duvoisin, R. (1950). *Petunia*. New York: Knopf.

Eastman, P.D. (1960). *Are you my mother?* New York: Random House.

Galdone, P. (1973). *The little red hen*. Boston, MA: Houghton Mifflin.

Lenski, L. (1965). *The little farm*. New York: Henry Z. Walek.

Piper, W. (1954). *The little engine that could*. New York: Platt & Munk.

Potter, B. (1902). *The tale of Peter Rabbit*. New York: Scholastic Book Services.

Zolotow, C. (1962). *Mr. Rabbit and the lovely present*. New York: Harper & Row.

Author Index

Page references followed by *f* indicate figures.

A

Adams, A., 7, 8, 9, 180
Adams, M.J., 66, 67, 180
Alvermann, D.E., 27, 180
Au, K., 63, 183

B

Bandura, A., 180
Bandy-Hedden, I., 13, 181
Barker, L.L., 22, 180
Barnard, H., 6, 180
Bellugi, U., 62, 180
Belmont, M., 185
Bemelmans, L., 68, 187
Biklen, S.K., 22, 180
Bloom, B., 62, 180
Bogdan, R., 22, 180
Bourgeois, P., 19, 187
Bredekamp, S., 7, 10, 180
Brown, M., 19, 107, 187
Brown, R., 62, 180
Bruner, J., 62, 180
Bruno, R., 7, 8, 9, 180
Bryant, D., 6, 7, 181

C

Calkins, L.M., 181
Carle, E., 107, 187

Cazden, C., 181
Chambers, W., 133, 136
Clark, M.M., 62, 181
Clay, M.M., 21, 57, 166, 181
Clifford, R., 6, 7, 181
Cohen, D., 63, 181
Cole, J., 133, 136
Copple, C., 10, 180
Corsaro, W., 22, 181
Cryan, J., 13, 181
Csikszentimihalyi, M., 181

D

DePaola, T., 93, 136, 187
Dewey, J., 87, 106, 181
Dillon, D.R., 27, 180
Durkin, D., 62, 181
Duvoisin, R., 93, 187

E

Eastman, P.D., 65, 122, 187
Eberts, M., 133
Erickson, H.L., 181

F

Feitelson, D., 63, 181
Fetterman, D.M., 22, 181
Field, T., 100, 181

Flemming, B.M., 132
Flesch, R., 7, 181
Forman, E., 181
Froebel, F., 6, 99, 181
Fromberg, D., 8, 10, 181, 182

G

Gable, C., 24, 187
Galda, L., 20, 63, 185
Galdone, P., 65, 93, 187
Gastright, J.F., 13, 184
Gilstrap, R., 9, 182
Goldstein, Z., 63, 181
Goodman, Y., 66, 69, 182
Gorton, H.B., 9, 182
Gough, P.B., 66, 183
Green, J.L., 22, 182
Griffith, P.L., 66, 183
Guba, E., 22, 183

H

Hamilton, D.S., 132
Harrison-McEachern, R., 13, 182
Hatcher, B., 14, 15, 182
Herman, B., 9, 10, 182
Hicks, J.D., 132
Hoban, R., 136
Hoffman, S.J., 63, 182
Holdaway, D., 59, 182
Holmes, C.T., 6, 7, 9, 14, 182
Hopkins, L.B., 136
Housden, T., 8, 182
Huberman, A.M., 27, 183
Humphrey, J.W., 13, 182
Hutchins, P., 136

I–J

Inhelder, B., 185
International Reading Association,
    59, 182
Johnson, C., 142

Johnson, D.W., 182
Johnson, N., 100, 183
Johnson, R.T., 182
Juel, C., 66, 183

K

Kam, R., 8, 182
Karweit, N., 12, 14, 183
King, C., 147
Kita, B., 63, 181
Krauss, R., 136

L

Lee, K., 24, 187
Lennenberg, E., 62, 183
Lenski, L., 93, 187
Lincoln, Y., 22, 183

M

Maehr, M.L., 183
Mandler, J., 100, 183
Mason, J., 63, 66, 183
McCaig, G., 10, 185
McCloskey, R., 136
McCombs, B.L., 183
McConnell, B.M., 6, 7, 9, 14, 182
McNeil, D., 62, 183
Menyuk, P., 62, 183
Miles, M.B., 27, 183
Monson, D., 19, 183
Montessori, M., 99, 100, 183
Moomgy, C., 24, 187
Moore, G., 100, 183
Morrow, L.M., 11, 19, 20, 57f, 62,
    63, 64, 66, 68, 89f, 97f, 100,
    102, 103f, 104, 104f, 105, 110f,
    183, 184, 186

N

Naron, N.K., 10, 184
Neuman, S., 100, 184

Nieman, R.H., 13, 184
Ninio, A., 63, 184

O

O'Brien, D.G., 27, 180
O'Connor, E.M., 19, 184
Oelerich, M., 7, 185
Ogle, D.M., 65, 185
Oldfather, P., 185

P

Peck, J., 10, 11, 12, 185
Pellegrini, A., 20, 63, 185
Peskin, M., 5, 6, 8, 9, 13, 14, 185
Piaget, J., 10, 11, 185
Piper, W., 187
Potter, B., 93, 187
Puleo, V., 6, 7, 9, 12, 14, 15, 185

R

Rand, M., 97, 100, 110*f*, 184, 185
Robinson, R.L., 9, 182
Roskos, K., 100, 184
Ross, E.D., 9, 185
Rothenberg, D., 8, 12, 185
Rusk, R., 99, 185

S

Sapp, M., 10, 185
Schickedanz, J., 102, 185
Schmidt, V., 15, 182
Scotland, J., 99, 185
Sebesta, S., 19, 183
Sendak, M., 147
Sharmat, M., 136
Sheehan, R., 13, 181

Skinner, E., 185
Smith, F., 59, 66, 186
Smith, J., 19, 20, 184
Strickland, D.S., 71, 77, 82, 186
Sulzby, E., 20, 58, 68, 186

T

Teale, W., 58, 62, 186
Terens, S., 14, 186
Thomson, P., 24, 187
Thorndyke, P., 20, 186
Towers, J.M., 14, 186
Turner, J.C., 186

U

U.S. Bureau of Census, 7, 9
U.S. Department of Commerce, 9, 186
U.S. Department of Education, 8, 186

V

Vygotsky, L.S., 10, 11, 58, 187

W

Wallat, C., 22, 182
Walsh, D., 14, 187
Washington, T., 24, 187
Webster, N.K., 7, 187
Weinstein, C.S., 104, 184
Westcott, N.B., 137
Wiechel, J., 13, 181
Wittrock, M.C., 187

Z

Zolotow, C., 105, 187

Subject Index

Page references followed by *t* or *f* indicate tables or figures, respectively.

A

ACCESSIBLE ENVIRONMENTAL PRINT, 102–105

ACHIEVEMENT, 14; literacy, 28, 29*t*, 49; reading, 13

ACTIVITIES: concepts about print, 137–139; culminating, 151–152; for developing positive attitudes, 140; follow-up, 65–66; in free-choice center time, 38–41; guided reading or listening, 64–65; in literacy center, 109; oral language, 139–140; for parents, 134; quiet, 113, 116, 118; sample unit, 136–152; student-initiated, 38–41; time spent in, 31–36. *See also* Literacy activities; *specific activities*

AFRICAN AMERICAN HISTORY (THEMATIC UNIT), 24

ALPHABET BOOKS: Nutrition Alphabetic Book activity, 139

ANALYSIS: implications, 49–55; observational data, 27–28; qualitative, 49–55; quantitative, 27–28, 49–55; results of, 27–48

ANECDOTAL OBSERVATIONS, 46–48, 52–53; samples, 169–179

ANIMAL UNIT: materials for, 106–109

ART: and literacy, 90–91; objectives, 146–147; sample unit, 146–147; at school and at home, 132–133; whole-group lesson outlines, 115, 117; whole-group lesson script, 126

ART ACTIVITIES: in free-choice center time, 40; sample unit, 146–147

ART CENTER: general materials for, 106; integrating literacy materials into, 106; materials for animal unit for, 106; preparing for sample unit, 135; whole-day script, 121, 124

ASSESSING LITERACY INSTRUCTION: objectives for, 72–75

ASSESSING PERFORMANCE, 81–82

ASSESSMENT MEASURES, 153–168; means and standard deviations, 29*t*. *See also specific measures*

ASSISTANCE FROM PARENTS, 133–134

ATTITUDES, POSITIVE: activities, 140–141; developing, 140–141; objectives, 72–75, 140–141

AUTHORS ACTIVITY, 141–142

AUTHOR'S SPOT: checklist for evaluating, 101*f*–102*f*. *See also* Writing Center

B

"BACK TO THE BASICS" MOVEMENT, 7

BIG BOOK ACTIVITY, 141

BIG BOOKS, 65

BLOCK AREA. *See* Block-Play Center

BLOCK CORNER. *See* Block-Play Center

BLOCK PLAY: in free-choice center time, 40; Where We Get Food activity, 145–146

BLOCK-PLAY CENTER: general materials for, 108; integrating literacy materials into, 108–109; materials for animal unit for, 108–109; preparing for sample unit, 135; whole-day script, 124–125

BOOKS: Big Book activity, 141; list and suggested activities, 136–137; My Nutrition Counting Book activity, 151; Nutrition Alphabetic Book activity, 139; Shaped Nutrition Books activity, 145; shared book reading, 65

BOOKS, CONCEPTS ABOUT: activities, 141–142; objectives, 73, 141–142; sample unit, 141–142

BULLETIN BOARDS: Notice Bulletin Board activity, 143–144

C

CALIFORNIA ACHIEVEMENT TEST, 14

CENTER TIME FOR SPECIAL PROJECTS: whole-day outline, 115; whole-day script, 126–127

CHALKTALK: *Mr. Rabbit and the Lovely Present* Chalktalk activity, 141

CHICKEN SOUP ACTIVITY, 147–148

CHILD INTERVIEWS, 41–46; summary, 51–52

CHILDREN'S READING ABILITY AND INTEREST IN READING: Teacher Rating Scale, 19, 21, 28, 29*t*, 165

CHILD'S CORNER, 134

CIRCLE TIME: half-day outline, 117; whole-day outline, 115; whole-day script, 127

CLASSROOMS: arranging, 100–102; floor plan, 103*f*; half-day program, 24–25; literacy-rich, 109–111; practice implications, 54; preparing for sample unit, 134–137; quality characteristics, 53; whole-day program, 25–26

COMPREHENSION: activities, 142–143; anecdotal observations, 169–173; development while storybook reading, 169–173; objectives, 73, 142–143; Probed Recall Listening Comprehension Test, 19, 29*t*, 158–161; sample unit, 142–143; through story retelling, 40

COMPREHENSION STRATEGIES, 31, 50, 128; time spent in, 29*t*, 32*t*, 34*t*, 36

COMPREHENSIVE TESTS OF BASIC SKILLS (CTBS), 13

CONFERENCE TIME, 84

CONFERENCES, 122–123

CONTENT AREAS: anecdotal observations, 173–175; integrating literacy into, 87–97, 173–175; integrating literacy materials into, 105–109

CONTENT-AREA LEARNING CENTERS: checklist for evaluating, 102*f*

CONTENT-AREA LITERACY, 31, 50; time spent in, 29*t*, 33*t*, 35*t*, 36

CONTENT-ORIENTED DRAMATIC PLAY, 109–111

COUNTING "EGGSACTLY" ACTIVITY, 151

COUNTRY OF THE WEEK ACTIVITY, 149–150

CRITICAL ACTIVITIES, 143

CTBS. *See* Comprehensive Tests of Basic Skills

CULMINATING ACTIVITY: activities, 152; objective, 151; sample unit, 151–152

CURRICULUM: framework for, 71–86; integrating literacy activities throughout, 87–90; literacy, 71–86

CURRICULUM WEBS, 96*f*, 97

D

DAILY PLANNING, 112–127; daily schedule planning sheet, 88, 89*f*; half-day outline, 116–117; whole-day outline, 113–115; whole-day script, 117–127

DAILY REVIEW: half-day outline, 117; whole-day outline, 115; whole-day script, 127

DARREN (STUDENT), 122; story, 56, 57*f*

DATA, OBSERVATIONAL: analysis of, 27–28; collecting, 21–22; results, 28–36, 50–51

DEMOGRAPHICS, 7–8

DESCRIBING GAME ACTIVITY, 139

DRAMATIC PLAY: content-oriented, 109–111; in free-choice center time, 40; Health-Food Restaurant activity, 145; World Dining activity, 146

DRAMATIC PLAY CENTER: general materials for, 108; integrating literacy materials into, 108; materials for animal unit for, 108; preparing for sample unit, 134; whole-day script, 124

E

EARLY LITERACY: program strategies & structures, 75, 76*f*; research, 61–69

ECOLOGY/POLLUTION (THEMATIC UNIT), 24

EGG ART ACTIVITY, 146

EMERGENT LITERACY: definition of, 57–58; perspectives of, 56–70

EMERGENT READING: Kindergarten Inventory of Concepts About Print and Emergent Reading, 19, 21, 28, 29*t*, 166

ENVIRONMENTAL PRINT ACTIVITY, 138

ENVIRONMENTS: checklist for evaluating, 101*f*–102*f*; classroom, 100–102, 103*f*, 134–137; literacy-rich, 69, 98–111; visually accessible print in, 102–105

F

FAMILY (THEMATIC UNIT), 24
FEATURED LETTERS ACTIVITY, 138
FIRE SAFETY (THEMATIC UNIT), 24
FLOOR PLANS, 103*f*
FOLLOW-UP ACTIVITIES, 65–66
FOOD(S) : Chicken Soup activity, 147–148; empty calorie foods, 131; Health-Food Restaurant activity, 145; how people prepare and eat, 131–132; importance of, 130; junk foods, 131; Making Applesauce activity, 150; "Oats, Peas, Beans" Song and Dance activity, 148; recipe for making butter, 126–127; Sort a Food activity, 151; sources of, 131; Where We Get Food activity, 145–146; World Dining activity, 146
FOOD COLLAGE ACTIVITY, 147
FOOD GROUPS, 130–132
FOOD WEBS, 141*f*
FOOD-GROUP WEBS ACTIVITY, 140
FREE-CHOICE CENTER TIME. *See* Free-choice period
FREE-CHOICE PERIOD: anecdotal observations, 179; half-day outline, 117; literacy activities in, 39–40; student-initiated activities in, 38–41; in whole-day and half-day kindergartens, 38, 39*t*; whole-day outline, 115; whole-day script, 124–125
FRIENDS (THEMATIC UNIT), 24

G

GAMES: Describing Game activity, 139; in free-choice center time, 40
GOLDILOCKS AND THE THREE BEARS PROP STORY ACTIVITY, 140
GROUPING PRACTICES, 82–83
GUIDED READING AND WRITING, 77–79; half-day outline, 116–117; lesson, 121–122; whole-day outline, 114–115; whole-day script, 121–123
GUIDED READING OR LISTENING ACTIVITIES, 64–65
GYM. *See* Outdoor play

H

HALF-DAY KINDERGARTEN: child interviews concerning, 45–46; classroom program, 24–25; free-choice center time in, 38, 39*t*; issues concerning, 5–16; literacy activities in, 28–31, 29*t*, 31–36, 34*t*–35*t*; literacy instruction in, 1–4; literacy materials used in, 41; observation sheet for,

154–155; organizational structures used in, 37*t*, 37–41; organizing for, 112–127; outline, 116–117; program, 115–117; research review, 12–14; teachers' responses to questionnaire, 42–43. *See also* Kindergarten

HANSEL AND GRETEL ACTIVITY, 149

HEALTH-FOOD RESTAURANT ACTIVITY, 145

HISTORICAL PERSPECTIVES, 5–7

HOME: art at, 132–133; literacy at, 133; science at, 133

HOME INFLUENCES, 62–63; research, 62–63

I

ILLUSTRATORS ACTIVITY, 142

IMAGINATIVE PLAY: in free-choice center time, 40

IMPLEMENTING UNITS: guidelines for, 95, 97

INDEPENDENT READING-WRITING PERIOD ACTIVITY, 140

INDEPENDENT WORK: half-day outline, 116–117; reading and writing, 79–81; whole-day outline, 114–115; whole-day program, 114–115; whole-day script, 121–123

INDIVIDUAL CONFERENCES, 122–123

INDIVIDUAL INSTRUCTION, 83–84

INDIVIDUAL NEEDS: organizing instructional settings to meet, 82–85

INSTRUCTION: content-area teaching, 87–97; guided reading and writing lessons, 121–122; individual, 83–84; introductory lessons, 137; theoretical framework for, 10–12; whole-group lessons, 115, 117, 123–124, 126. *See also* Literacy instruction

INSTRUCTIONAL SETTINGS: organizing, 82–85

INTEGRATED UNITS: benefits of, 95

INTEGRATING LITERACY, 87–97

INTEGRATING LITERACY ACTIVITIES, 87–90

INTEGRATING LITERACY MATERIALS, 105–109

INTEREST IN READING: Teacher Rating Scale, 19, 21, 28, 29*t*, 165

INTERNATIONAL READING ASSOCIATION COMMITTEE ON LITERACY DEVELOPMENT IN EARLY CHILDHOOD: literacy acquisition statement, 59–60

INTERVIEW QUESTIONS, 167

INTERVIEWS: child, 41–46, 51–52; teacher, 41–46, 51; Teacher Interview, 167–168

INTRODUCTORY LESSONS: morning message, 137; sample unit, 137

INVENTED SPELLING, 68

J

JENNIFER (STUDENT), 123

JIM (STUDENT), 122–123

JOURNAL WRITING ACTIVITY, 144

K

KINDERGARTEN: attendance, 7–8; curriculum goals, 22–23; definition of, 5; demographics, 7–8; historical perspectives and, 5–7; length of school day, 7–8; public-school, 6; reasons children should attend, 5–6; research implications for, 61–69; storybook reading strategies for, 64–65; study program, 22–26. *See also* Half-day kindergarten; Whole-day kindergarten

KINDERGARTEN INVENTORY OF CONCEPTS ABOUT PRINT AND EMERGENT READING, 19; Checklist, 166; literacy achievement results, 28; means and standard deviations, 29*t*; procedure, 21

KINDERGARTEN POLICIES–WHAT IS BEST FOR CHILDREN? (NAEYC), 10

KNOWLEDGE ABOUT PRINT, 66–67, 128; research, 66–67

KNOWLEDGE ABOUT PRINT ACTIVITIES, 30, 50; time spent in, 29*t*, 32*t*, 34*t*, 36

K-W-L STRATEGY, 65

L

LANGUAGE ARTS LESSONS: half-day outline, 117; whole-day outline, 115; whole-group, 115, 117, 126

LANGUAGE DEVELOPMENT: literacy objectives for, 72

LEARNING: self-directed, 84–85

LEARNING CENTERS: content-area, 102*f*. *See also specific centers*

LEMONADE STAND ACTIVITY, 146

LENGTH OF SCHOOL DAY: demographics, 7–8

LESSONS: guided reading and writing, 121–122; introductory, 137; whole-group, 115, 117, 123–124, 126

LETTERS: Featured Letters activity, 138

LIBRARY CORNER, 104–105; book list and suggested activities, 136–137; checklist for evaluating, 101*f*; preparing for sample unit, 136

THE LIBRARY CORNER ACTIVITY, 140

LISTENING: activities in free-choice center time, 39; guided, 64–65; Probed Recall Listening Comprehension Test, 19, 29*t*, 158; receptive, 72

LITERACY: art and, 90–91; content-area, 29*t*, 31, 33*t*, 35*t*, 36, 50; early, 61–69; emergent, 56–58; integration into content areas, 87–97, 173–175; materials, 41; mathematics and, 94–95; music and, 91; objectives, 72–75; play and, 91–92; roots of, 66; at school and at home, 133; science and, 92–94; social studies and, 92–94

LITERACY ACHIEVEMENT: data results, 49; measures, 29*t*, 153–168; results, 28. *See also specific measures*

LITERACY ACQUISITION SKILLS, 59–61

LITERACY ACTIVITIES: in free-choice center time, 39–40; integrating throughout curriculum, 87–90; observation sheets for recording, 154–157; time spent in, 31–36, 34*t*–35*t*; in whole-day and half-day kindergartens, 28–31, 29*t*. *See also specific activities*

LITERACY CENTER, 103–105, 104*f*; activities in, 109; checklist for evaluating, 101*f*; morning gathering in, 114, 116, 118–121; preparing for sample unit, 135–136

LITERACY INSTRUCTION: in half- and whole-day kindergarten, 1–4; organizational structures used in, 37*t*, 37–41; preparing and assessing, 72–75

LITERACY INTEGRATED INTO CONTENT AREAS, 128–129

LITERACY MATERIALS, 41; integrating into content areas, 105–109

LITERACY-CENTER TIME: strategies to facilitate, 79–80; whole-day outline, 115; whole-day script, 125–126

LITERACY-ENRICHED THEMATIC PLAY, 110–111; additional ideas for, 110*f*

LITERACY-RICH ENVIRONMENTS, 69; creating framework for, 98–111; observations in, 109–111; perspectives concerning, 99–100; research, 69

LITERAL ACTIVITY, 143

M

MACARONI ART ACTIVITY, 147

MAIL: Nutritional Mail Service activity, 145

MAKING APPLESAUCE ACTIVITY, 150

MATERIALS: for animal unit, 106, 108–109; for Art Center, 106; for Block-Play Center, 108; for Dramatic Play Center, 108; literacy, 105–109; for Math Center, 107; for Music Center, 106; for Science Center, 107; for Social Studies Center, 107–108

MATH: activities, 151; and literacy, 94–95; objectives, 151; sample unit, 151; whole-group lesson, 115, 117, 123–124, 126

MATH CENTER: in free-choice center time, 40; general materials for, 107; integrating literacy materials into, 107; materials for animal unit for, 107; preparing for sample unit, 135; whole-day script, 121

MORNING GATHERING: half-day outline, 116; whole-day outline, 114; whole-day script, 118–121

MORNING MESSAGE: activity, 137; objective, 137; sample unit, 137

MOSTLY ME: OUR BODIES (THEMATIC UNIT), 24

MR. RABBIT AND THE LOVELY PRESENT CHALKTALK ACTIVITY, 141

MUSIC: activities, 147–148; and literacy, 91; objectives, 147–148; sample unit, 147–148; whole-group lesson, 115, 117, 126

MUSIC CENTER: general materials for, 106; integrating literacy materials into, 106; materials for animal unit for, 106; preparing for sample unit, 135

MY NUTRITION COUNTING BOOK ACTIVITY, 151

N

NAEYC. *See* National Association for the Education of Young Children

NATIONAL ASSOCIATION FOR THE EDUCATION OF YOUNG CHILDREN (NAEYC), 10, 49, 128

NEWSLETTER TO PARENTS ABOUT NUTRITION, 132–134

NOTICE BULLETIN BOARD ACTIVITY, 143–144

NUTRITION ALPHABETIC BOOK ACTIVITY, 139

NUTRITION UNIT (SAMPLE), 24, 130–152; art, 146–147; comprehension, 142–143; concepts about books, 141–142; concepts about print, 137–139; culminating activity, 151–152; curriculum web for, 96*f*, 97; introductory lessons: morning message, 137; Library Corner book list and suggested activities for, 136–137; math, 151; music, 147–148; newsletter to parents, 132–134; oral language, 139–140; play, 145–146; preparing classroom for, 134–137; science, 150; social studies, 148–150; writing, 143–145

NUTRITIONAL MAIL SERVICE ACTIVITY, 145

O

"OATS, PEAS, BEANS" SONG AND DANCE ACTIVITY, 148

OBSERVATIONAL DATA: analysis of, 27–28; collecting, 21–22; results, 28–36; results from, 50–51

OBSERVATIONS: anecdotal, 46–48, 52–53, 169–179; in literacy-rich classroom, 109–111

OBSERVING TEACHERS: directions for, 153; sample entry, 153–154; sheet for half-day kindergarten, 154–155; sheet for whole-day kindergarten, 156–157

ORAL LANGUAGE, 61–62; anecdotal observations, 173–175; objectives, 72, 139; research, 61–62; sample unit, 139–140

ORAL LANGUAGE ACTIVITIES, 31, 50, 128, 139–140; time spent in, 29*t*, 33*t*, 35*t*, 36

ORGANIZATION, 112–127; to meet individual needs, 82–85; structures for, 37*t*, 37–41

OUTDOOR PLAY: half-day outline, 117; Lemonade Stand activity, 146; preparing for sample unit, 135; whole-day outline, 115; whole-day script, 125

P

PARENTS: activities for, 134; newsletter about nutrition to, 132–134

PEABODY, ELIZABETH, 6

PERFORMANCE OF READING AND WRITING ACCOMPLISHMENTS: assessing, 81–82

PERFORMANCE OF TASKS COMPLETED: half-day outline, 117; whole-day outline, 115; whole-day script, 127

PET SHOW (THEMATIC UNIT), 24

PLANNING: daily, 88, 89*f*, 112–127; guidelines for, 95, 97

PLANTING ACTIVITY, 150

PLANTS (THEMATIC UNIT), 24

PLAY: activities, 145–146; block, 40, 108–109; dramatic, 40, 108–111, 145–146; imaginative, 40; and literacy, 91–92; objectives, 145–146; outdoor, 117, 125, 135, 146; sample unit, 145–146; thematic, 110*f*, 110–111

POETRY: Poetry Reading activity, 142; Webbing and Creating Poetry activity, 143

POSITIVE ATTITUDES: activities, 140–141; developing, 140–141; objectives, 72–75, 140–141

POTATO GROWTH ACTIVITY, 150

PRACTICE, 1–4; classroom, 54; emergent literacy perspectives, 56–70; grouping, 82–83; research implications for, 69–70; theoretical framework for, 10–12; in whole-day kindergarten, 10–12

PREPARING AND ASSESSING LITERACY INSTRUCTION, 72–75

PRETEND WRITING, 20

PRINT: Environmental Print activity, 138; visually accessible environmental, 102–105

PRINT, CONCEPTS ABOUT: activities, 137–139; Kindergarten Inventory of Concepts About Print and Emergent Reading, 19, 21, 28, 29*t*, 166; objectives, 74, 137–139; sample unit, 137–139

PRINT, KNOWLEDGE ABOUT, 66–67; activities related to, 29*t*, 30, 32*t*, 34*t*, 36; anecdotal observations, 176–179; research, 66–67

PRINT-AWARENESS ACTIVITIES: in free-choice center time, 39

PRIVATE SPOTS, 80

PROBED RECALL LISTENING COMPREHENSION TEST, 19; directions for administering, 158; means and standard deviations, 29*t*; procedure, 19

PROBED RECALL LISTENING COMPREHENSION TEST: *ARTHUR'S EYES*, 160–161

PROBED RECALL LISTENING COMPREHENSION TEST: *FRANKLIN IN THE DARK*: structural section, 158–159; traditional section, 159

PROJECTS: center time for, 115, 126–127

PROP STORIES: *Goldilocks and the Three Bears* Prop Story activity, 140

PUBLIC-SCHOOL KINDERGARTENS, 6. *See also* Half-day kindergarten; Kindergarten; Whole-day kindergarten

Q

QUALITATIVE ANALYSIS: implications, 49–55; results, 27–48

QUANTITATIVE ANALYSIS, 27–28; implications, 49–55; results, 27–48

QUESTIONNAIRE: half-day teachers' responses to, 42–43; whole-day teachers' responses to, 43–45

QUIET ACTIVITIES: half-day outline, 116; whole-day outline, 113; whole-day script, 118

R

READING: anecdotal observations, 169–173; arranging classrooms to motivate, 100–102; guided, 64–65, 77–79, 114–117, 121–123; independent, 79–81; literacy objectives for, 72–75; performance of accomplishments, 81–82; Poetry Reading activity, 142; positive attitudes toward, 72–75;

shared book, 65; shared writing and, 77; storybook, 63–66, 169–173; Teacher Rating Scale, 19, 21, 28, 29*t*, 165; types of experiences, 75–81

READING ACHIEVEMENT, 13

READING ACTIVITIES: in free-choice center time, 39

READING ALOUD AND RESPONDING, 75–77

RECEPTIVE LISTENING: literacy objectives for, 72

RECIPE FOR MAKING BUTTER, 126–127

REENACTMENT. *See* Story Reenactment Test

REPEATING STORIES, 65

RESEARCH, 1–4; early literacy, 61–69; emergent literacy perspectives, 56–70; home influences, 62–63; implications, 14–15, 54–55, 69–70; knowledge of print, 66–67; limitations, 14–15; literacy-rich environments, 69; oral language, 61–62; review, 12–14; storybook reading, 63–64; summary, 69–70; writing, 67–68

RESEARCH STUDY: assessment measures, 29*t*, 153–168; data analysis, 27–28; kindergarten program, 22–26; methods, 18–22; observational data collection, 21–22; procedures, 18–21; purpose, 17–18; questions, 17–18; subjects, 18

RESULTS: literacy achievement, 28, 49; from observational data, 28–36, 50–51

RETELLING: story, 40, 65; Story Retelling activity, 139; Story Retelling Test, 19–20, 28, 29*t*, 162–163

REVIEW OF THE DAY: half-day outline, 117; whole-day outline, 115; whole-day script, 127

RHYMES: Singing Rhymes activity, 148

S

SCHOOL DAY: daily schedule planning sheet, 88, 89*f*; half-day outline, 116–117; half-day program, 24–25; length of, 7–8; whole-day outline, 113–115; whole-day program, 25–26; whole-day script, 117–127

SCHURZ, MARGARET, 6

SCIENCE: activities, 150; and literacy, 92–94; objectives, 150; sample unit, 150; at school and at home, 133; whole-group lesson, 115, 117, 126

SCIENCE CENTER: general materials for, 107; integrating literacy materials into, 107; materials for animal unit for, 107; preparing for sample unit, 135; whole-day script, 125

THE SEA (THEMATIC UNIT), 24

SEED EXPLORING ACTIVITY, 150

SELF-DIRECTED LEARNING, 84–85

SETTINGS: organizing, 82–85

SHAPED NUTRITION BOOKS ACTIVITY, 145

SHARED BOOK READING EXPERIENCES, 65

SHARED WRITING AND READING, 77

SHOW AND TELL ACTIVITY, 139

SINGING RHYMES ACTIVITY, 148

SKILLS: in literacy acquisition, 59–61

SOCIAL STUDIES: activities, 148–150; and literacy, 92–94; objectives, 148–149; sample unit, 148–150; whole-group lesson, 115, 117, 126

SOCIAL STUDIES CENTER: general materials for, 107–108; integrating literacy materials into, 107–108; materials for animal unit for, 108; preparing for sample unit, 135; whole-day script, 125

SORT A FOOD ACTIVITY, 151

SORT BY SOUND ACTIVITY, 137–138

SPECIAL PROJECTS: center time for, 115, 126–127

SPELLING: invented, 68

SPRING (THEMATIC UNIT), 24

STONE SOUP ACTIVITY, 148

STORIES: repeated, 65

STORY REENACTMENT TEST, 19, 164–165; literacy achievement results, 28; means and standard deviations, 29t; procedure, 20–21

STORY RETELLING, 65; in free-choice center time, 40

STORY RETELLING ACTIVITY, 139

STORY RETELLING TEST, 19; administering, 162; literacy achievement results, 28; means and standard deviations, 29t; oral and written, 163; procedure, 19–20

STORY STRUCTURE ACTIVITY, 142

STORYBOOK READING, 63–66; anecdotal observations, 169–173; research, 63–64; strategies for kindergarten, 64–65

STORYBOOK READING ACTIVITIES, 30, 50, 128; time spent in, 29t, 32t, 34t, 35–36

STUDENT-INITIATED ACTIVITIES: in free-choice center time, 38–41

T

TEACHER INTERVIEWS, 41–46; responses, 51; Teacher Interview, 167–168

TEACHER RATING SCALE, 19, 165; literacy achievement results, 28; means and standard deviations, 29t; procedure, 21

TEACHERS: directions for observing, 153; half-day, 42–43; whole-day, 43–45

TEACHING: content-area, 87–97

TEXT COMPREHENSION. See Comprehension

THEMATIC PLAY: literacy-enriched, 110f, 110–111

THEMATIC UNITS. See Units

THEORETICAL FRAMEWORK, 10–12

THE THREE BILLY GOATS GRUFF ACTIVITY, 149

TITLE I, 13–14

TRANSPORTATION (THEMATIC UNIT), 24

U

UNITS: curriculum web for, 96*f*, 97; guidelines for planning and implementing, 95, 97; integrated, 95; sample materials, 106–109; samples, 24, 130–152

V

VEGETABLE PRINT PAINTING ACTIVITY, 146
VERY-OWN WORDS ACTIVITY, 138

W

WEBBING AND CREATING POETRY ACTIVITY, 143
WEBS: curriculum, 96*f*, 97; example, 144*f*
WHAT'S FOR LUNCH? (THEMATIC UNIT), 24
WHERE WE GET FOOD ACTIVITY, 145–146
"WHOLE CHILD" PHILOSOPHY, 7
WHOLE-DAY KINDERGARTEN: child interviews concerning, 45–46; classroom program, 25–26; free-choice center time in, 38, 39*t*; issues concerning, 5–16; literacy activities in, 28–31, 29*t*, 31–36, 32*t*–33*t*; literacy activities in free-choice center time in, 39–40; literacy instruction in, 1–4; literacy materials used in, 41; observation sheet for, 156–157; organizational structures used in, 37*t*, 37–41; organizing for, 112–127; outline, 113–115; renewed interest in, 8–9; research review, 12–14; script, 117–127; teachers' responses to questionnaire, 43–45; theoretical framework for, 10–12. *See also* Kindergarten
WHOLE-GROUP LESSONS, 115, 117, 123–124, 126
WORDS: Very-own Words activity, 138
WORLD DINING ACTIVITY, 146
WRITING, 67–68; arranging classrooms to motivate, 100–102; guided, 77–79, 114–117, 121–123; independent, 79–81; objectives, 72–75, 143–145; performance of accomplishments, 81–82; pretend, 20; research, 67–68; sample unit, 143–145; shared, 77; types of experiences, 75–81
WRITING ACTIVITIES, 31, 50, 128; anecdotal observations, 175–176; in free-choice center time, 40; Journal Writing activity, 144; sample unit, 143–145; time spent in, 29*t*, 32*t*–35*t*, 36
WRITING CENTER, 105; checklist for evaluating, 101*f*–102*f*; preparing for sample unit, 135–136
WRITING SAMPLE TEST, 19; means and standard deviations, 29*t*; procedure, 20